Contents

RITA ERNSTEIN

War Dancer

Memoirs of an ENSA Performer in World War II

Disclaimer

This book is based on a personal diary and memoirs. Recounting experiences as a young dancer touring with ENSA (Entertainments National Service Association) during World War II. The events, places, and people are described as the writer remembered them at the time, offering a first-hand perspective of life on the road during the war.

While every effort has been made to add accurate historical context as footnotes, some details may be subject to memory limitations, personal interpretation, or historical inconsistencies. Certain names, dates, and events may differ from official records or other historical accounts. This book is intended as a personal recollection rather than an exhaustive historical document.

Readers should consider the memoir as a subjective and lived experience, providing insight into a period of history through the eyes of someone who lived it rather than a definitive account of wartime events.

Second edition

ISBN: 978-1-7391645-1-5

This book was professionally typeset on Reedsy. Find out more at reedsy.com

Prologue

Every Night Something Awful? Not Quite!

If you ask any soldier who sat through an ENSA show during the war, they'll probably chuckle and say, "Ah, ENSA... Every Night Something Awful!" And yes, sometimes the stage was a wobbly wooden plank, the pianist might have had to make do with a missing key, and the comedian's punch line competing with the roar of a passing Spitfire. But ENSA wasn't just about the cabaret and comedians. It was about bringing a taste of home to the men and women who needed it most—wherever they were.

ENSA—the Entertainments National Service Association—was Britain's answer to a crucial wartime problem: how do you keep spirits high when people are fighting for their lives? The government decided that if the troops couldn't go to the theatre, the theatre would go to them. So, from 1939 onwards, actors, singers, dancers, and comedians packed their bags, left the bright lights of London behind, and set off to perform in some of the most unlikely venues imaginable—bomb shelters, jungle clearings, desert outposts, and even the decks of ships rocking in the middle of the ocean. They travelled to areas from Iceland to Burma, covering Northwestern Europe, Germany, West and North Africa, the Middle East, and the Indian subcontinent.

1

It wasn't glamorous. There were no luxury dressing rooms, and the audience was often a mix of exhausted soldiers, sceptical officers, and, as rumours go, the occasional wandering goat. But when the music started or the first joke landed, something magical happened. For a few precious moments, the war faded away. Laughter and applause replaced gunfire. Homesick men felt, just for a while, that they weren't so far from home. Between 1939 and 1946, ENSA produced 2,565,656 cinema shows and theatrical performances, entertaining allied forces with audiences estimated to exceed 500 million and artists regularly performing two shows a day.

In 1945, actors Laurence Olivier and Ralph Richardson were appointed honorary lieutenants in the Entertainments National Service Association (ENSA), embarking on a six-week tour of Europe, performing Shakespearean plays including "Arms and the Man," "Peer Gynt," and "Richard III". Although ENSA members were civilians, they were provided uniforms to reflect their service to the war effort. These uniforms were similar to the khaki green military style but lacked official ranks or military insignia. While not soldiers, ENSA performers were deeply embedded in military life, given officer status to allow them to use the officer's mess, and often travelled to front lines and military bases. Their uniform helped them to be recognised as part of the wider war effort and granted them access to military facilities for accommodation, food, recreation, and performance spaces. The ENSA founder, Basil Dean, was concerned that without a uniform, any captured performer may be mistaken as a spy.

This memoir contains first-hand stories written by one of

those young performers Rita Ernstein. Her diary entries detail her experiences alongside her sister Barbara, known as Betty, and together, they created the dance duo The Erwin Twins. With their troupe, they braved enemy fire, endured difficult conditions and lost loved ones. While touring they discovered that no matter how tough things got, the show had to go on.

The diary was discovered by Rita's son, along with old photographs and memorabilia in a suitcase shortly after her death at the age of 88. It had been stored unopened in an attic. In this edition, the prologue and introduction have been revised to provide additional historical context and some background information on Rita. The words of the memoirs remain untouched, allowing readers to immerse themselves in her unfiltered words. Footnotes have occasionally been added to clarify historical references, locations or events without disrupting the flow of her writing to ensure an authentic, uninterrupted memoir experience.

Introduction

Rita and Betty

These memoirs are a twelve-month, war-time diary of Rita Ernstein, which begins when she was 24 years of age. Born in Hull in 1919, Rita was a dancer in a duo with her sister Barbara, known as Betty. They trained locally and began making a name for themselves at local events and stage shows from the tender age of 7. Winning numerous competitions, they recognised their future lay in performance. They began their professional dancing careers before the war, touring theatres around the country as 'The Erwin Twins'.

The Erwin Twins - Rita & Betty

Before this diary begins, sisters Rita and Betty were performing with ENSA, bringing entertainment to wartime audiences. In the early months of 1944, while touring in venues around Darlington, Rita met John Stewart, a classical opera singer from Kent. Their shared passion for performance quickly drew them together, and amidst the turmoil of war, their romance blossomed. Despite their tours pulling them in different directions, each and every letter they exchanged only strengthened their connection. But in a world overshadowed by conflict, love was never simple.

Later that year, their paths crossed again in London at the Theatre Royal, Drury Lane, which served as ENSA's headquarters during World War II. By then, John—better known as Jack, and often referred to as J in the memoirs—was helping manage and organise ENSA's touring companies. It was here that their love rekindled, deepening into a profound and lasting connection. However, circumstances soon forced them apart. Jack continued touring with ENSA in North Africa, performing alongside some of the era's most notable entertainers, including stage, screen, and radio comedian Tommy Trinder, famous for his catchphrase, "You lucky people!"

In Rita's memoirs, we witness some of the harsh realities of life on the road with ENSA. Through Rita's eyes, we experience the challenging living conditions, the often gruelling travel arrangements, and the exhilarating yet exhausting pace of moving from town to town, bringing entertainment to the troops. Alongside

the hardships, the memoirs also capture the lighter moments—
the glamour of officers' parties, the friendships formed along
the way, the excitement of the new places and the fascinating
interactions with the military personnel they performed for.
As Rita's troupe passes through war-torn towns and Allied
encampments, their journey is not without heartbreak and
loss. In stark contrast to the laughter and music they worked
so hard to provide, interwoven with her story of love, Rita's
memoirs are continually devoted to her darling Jack until fate
intervenes and they meet again.

It is important to note that Rita and Betty were the daughters
of a highly respectable Jewish family in Hull. Their parents,
Rachael and Hirsch, (Hirsch is a Yiddish and Hebrew name,
often anglicised as Harry), had emigrated from a small Polish
village to England during the First World War. At that time,
in the early 1900s, Jewish communities in that region faced
escalating persecution. The deep hostility towards Jews forced
many families to flee for their safety, a situation poignantly
depicted in the musical and film 'Fiddler on the Roof'.

Rita and Betty with their mother

Against this historical backdrop, interfaith relationships faced intense disapproval, both within Jewish communities and beyond. While such relationships can still be challenging today, in the early 20th century, they often led to outright ostracisation. A well-known example of this struggle is portrayed in Neil Diamond's 'The Jazz Singer'. Rita's memoirs contain references to her own family's disapproval of such relationships. Sentiments that surface in letters she received from relatives while travelling abroad.

The following account has been faithfully transcribed from

Rita's original notebook by her son, Martin Stewart, with additional historical context provided by her granddaughter, Simone Baldwin. We are immensely proud of the part Rita played in the war effort and feel privileged to be able to read about her time in history.

1

December 1944

December 21st Thursday 1944

After a few hours fitful sleep in a bunk onboard the HMS St. Helier [1] which we boarded in Newhaven yesterday, Wednesday afternoon, we actually set sail at about 6.00am and had a very calm crossing. Breakfast at 7.40am and a good blow on deck and a game of lexicon with Kay and Edna until lunch. Stan Poute, the American Lieutenant I spent such a pleasant evening with yesterday, came into the ward room after lunch and we walked and talked till disembarkation at Dieppe at 3.00 pm. I promised to phone him if we ever work in Paris – a very charming American but nothing to touch my J. We had our passports checked at Dieppe and then had a

---

[1] HMS St. Helier was originally a passenger ferry. In 1940, during World War II, she was requisitioned by the Royal Navy. The journey from Newhaven to Dieppe was a common route for Allied forces, this route was a critical supply and personnel link between England and the European mainland during the latter stages of the war.

beautiful meal at the hostel, after which we travelled by truck to Rouen. [2] The hostel here is a beautiful old house, the staff are most obliging and we are beginning to feel excited. Another lovely meal interspersed with plenty of friendly patter – and so to bed. Very tired but rather happy. A good night's sleep will do me good and tomorrow I must write to Jack, bless him.

Good night.

December 23rd Saturday 1944

Set out from Rouen at 8.00 am and travelled to Lille. We stopped for a snack at 11.45 am at Amiens and from there passed through Neuf-Chattelle, Leuven and Doullen – all of which are practically nothing but rubble heaps. I've never seen such devastation, by comparison, even in England!

Arrived at Lille at about 5.30 pm frozen stiff, hungry and very weary indeed. We are staying in The Hotel Royal the night and travelling to Brussels tomorrow morning. This evening we all

---

[2] Rouen, France, was liberated by Canadian forces in August 1944. Although there is very little information about specific ENSA performances, the presence of Allied troops in the city after its liberation created ample entertainment opportunities. Following the Normandy landings, Rouen became an important strategic hub, with a steady movement of military units through the area.

Among the first Allied units to enter Rouen was R Force, a British deception unit tasked with misleading German forces. Along with other military detachments, their presence would have provided ENSA performers with an ever-changing audience, eager for an element of normalcy amid the chaos of wartime France.

went to an officer's club [3] and started the evening on champagne with Bill, a Canadian officer who was also staying at The Royal (I made a silent toast to Jack with my first drink), after dinner we met Bill again and we all went to a night club. I went with Stewart Hayword, an R.E. Captain, with whom Betsy, Betty and I spent a pleasant evening with more champagne. We left about 12.15 am when the gendarmerie arrived!! It's been a beautiful Xmassy day and apart from the long journey, most enjoyable. Stewart is a lot like Jack but still can't touch him! If we continue as well as we started this is going to be an exceptional tour. I'm terribly sleepy – Goodnight.

December 24th Sunday 1944

Xmas eve. I'm still writing in bed at 11.15 pm in a very nice bedroom with bathroom combined. We arrived at the ENSA hostel in Brussels, at approximately 2.30 this afternoon after travelling by road in the same van with Rhyme & Rhythm Co. from Lille. Commenced the journey at 10.30 am. Beautiful fine day but freezing cold – my feet felt as though they would break off before we reached our destination. We stopped at a little town just inside the Belgium border for morning coffee, then continued uneventfully to Brussels. We were disappointed to

---

[3] Lille was liberated from German occupation on September 4, 1944, by British forces. During the war, the British military established Officers' Clubs as a place for officers to unwind, whether they were stationed in the area or just passing through. These clubs provided much-needed comforts—good food, a place to sleep, and a social hub where soldiers could relax, share stories, and escape, if only briefly, from the realities of war.

learn on arrival here that Carol Lewis is playing in Brussels, and that we shall be on the road again tomorrow – Xmas day to Eindhoven in Holland – very near the Jerry's. We shall be working there tomorrow night, all being well. After lunch, we unpacked as much as necessary, had a very welcome bath and then amused ourselves in the lounge – had a few glasses of dubonnet – a sweet wine. Dinner, wrote a long letter to Jack which I hope will pass the censor! Played a game of rummy with Kay and so to bed, exceptionally tired. A short air raid warning but no activity. I do wish we'd been staying here, I very much like the look of Brussels, but perhaps we shall work back this way and perhaps also visit Paris. Betsy, Edna and Vivienne accepted an invitation to a party at the house of a Belgian family – I hope they are enjoying themselves. I'm feeling very homesick for J at the present moment.

December 25th Monday 1944

We were supposed to be on the road by 9 am today, but as the transport was held up, Betty, Betsy, Mona and I had a look at the Brussels shops and went into a café at the corner of the street for a coffee – it cost us 25 francs each – aghast at that! One pays for experience. We eventually commenced our journey at 11.45 am passed through Rijen, which is badly blitzed and stopped at Diest for a snack. The café proprietor provided the soup, and we supplied corned beef and bread – our Xmas dinner!

Dec. 25th 1944 Xmas Day.

We were supposed to be on the road
by 9.a.m. today, but as the
transport was held up, Betty, Betsy
Mona & I had a look at the Brussels
shops & went into a café at the
corner of the street for a coffee — it
cost us 25 francs each — expensive
at that! One pays for experience.
We eventually commenced our
journey at 11.45 — Passed through
Louvain which is badly blitzed &
stopped at Diest for a snack. The
café proprietor provided the soup
we supplied corned beef & bread —
our Xmas dinner!
I was struck by the good
Belgian houses & buildings, more
built to pattern but so charmingly
designed & gaily painted. We also
bought sweets at Diest which cost
the equivalent of 1/- for a small
bar of nougat.
On again, we passed over the
famous Albert Canal where bitter fighting
has taken place both in this war
& the last & I saw little crosses
marking the graves of men from

Extract from Rita's diary

14

I was struck by the Belgian houses and buildings, none built to pattern but so charmingly designed and gaily painted. We also bought sweets at Diest, which cost the equivalent of 1/- for a small bag of nougat. [4] On again, we passed over the famous James Albert canal where bitter fighting has taken place, both in this war and the last and I saw little crosses marking the graves of men from both sides who have died. Over the Brighton Bridge, which had been re-constructed three times and then across the frontier into Holland. The weather has been fine but so cold that the ponds are frozen hard and we saw the children skating as we sped by. The Holland homes are even more attractive than those in Belgium, as quaint and brightly painted despite the blitzing. We arrived at Eindhoven at 3.30 pm and had a marvellous surprise. The welfare office[5] welcomed us with open arms – we had a marvellous welcome and real Xmas fare – turkey and wine and we felt much better after that. We were taken to a camp near the front line to a party where we gave a short floor show and the boys really loved it.

---

[4] Nougat is a chewy, sweet confection made from sugar or honey, whipped egg whites, and nuts (like almonds or pistachios). It often has a light, airy texture and can include dried fruit or chocolate. Popular in Europe, it comes in soft and hard varieties, with the soft version being more chewy and the hard version more brittle.

[5] During World War II, the Welfare Office supported the well-being and logistical needs of military personnel, which also included the ENSA troupes. When performers arrived at new bases, the Welfare Office helped them find accommodation. They also arranged meals, ensuring the performers had the energy to keep spirits high. The Welfare Office coordinated transport to get ENSA teams to their performance venues on time. They worked closely with commanding officers to schedule performances, ensuring that as many troops as possible could enjoy a break from the harsh realities of war.

Actually, we were only six miles from the front and the boys were due back at dawn tomorrow morning. After the show we were pleasantly entertained in the officer's mess and at about 12.30 pm, we started the homeward journey. We were seven in one car, and we'd gone about four miles when the engine gave out, we were stranded in the petrifying cold for over two hours and the poor driver took the engine to bits about four times in vain. By about 3.00 am, we were eventually picked up by one of the other cars. Brandy helped to revive us slightly, and we crawled into bed about 4.00 am. And that ends the first day and night in Eindhoven. However, we did entertain the boys and every time, I was almost gassed by stale beer breath – I seemed to attract it! We really did our duty bravely, and I was glad. I have forgotten to write that we are entertaining the 2nd army in this area. There is constant gunfire and tonight a buzz bomb was dropped in Eindhoven.

December 26th Tuesday 1944

A beautiful sunny day but freezing cold, have caught a very severe cold as a result of our exposure last night – nevertheless, I feel much better after a hot bath. I have been busy all morning getting organised for the show. At lunchtime, the Halle Orchestra arrived at the hostel, 76 in all, and we all had an eventful lunch. The people of Holland, in company of those in France, are starving; they have plenty of money but nothing to buy, and the barter and exchange system plays a very important part in life now. Our first show at the Rembrandt Theatre (GT-Grand Theatre) a very good theatre, but without heat and we were freezing all the time; a pool of water in our dressing room was covered in ice! The show went well and afterwards we were invited by RAF officers to a party. I enjoyed it very much but all the time I was wishing I was talking and dancing with J instead of the Wing Commander I was with. He was very charming but it's no good at all. One of the officers promised to get me some Brussels lace. Crawled into bed at 3.30 am, where I am writing this. Goodnight.

December 27th Wednesday 1944

Came to life very late – washed my hair and had lunch and went to the theatre for the matinee. There is practically no heating at all and our dressing rooms upstairs are like frozen ponds, the water has dripped from the cracked pipes and frozen. We worked the matinee in our little dress and were still cold. The welfare officer told us today that no girl should go out in the streets alone but must always be accompanied by a man. The reason for this is that German para-troops have been dropped in the town, but fortunately they were caught dressed up as military police. The evening show was good and all our RAF friends were in the front row and afterwards took us back to their mess, a converted monastery and we had a lovely quiet party. There were Bill and Edna, Harry and Betty, Jim and Vivienne, Steve and myself and at Midnight they all wished me happy birthday with a champagne toast. Then Marjorie, who was with Tig, played the piano and we all danced. We arrived back at the hostel at about 2.30 am and we had my birthday cake. A simply lovely evening but dearly missing you! I'm 25 now and I hope you are thinking of me too. Goodnight and God bless.

December 28th Thursday 1944 – My Birthday

Awoke at about 10.30 am and went out with Betty and the RAF padre[6] Mr Ward to Phillips, where he bought us each a lovely little dynamo torch. He insisted on us accepting the gift as a token of his pleasure in meeting us and we were very touched. He's such a sweet man. I also bought a very good electric razor for Jack – a perfectly neat affair which I'm sure he'll like. I gave the salesman a box of cigarettes and some toilet soap and he was delighted. After lunch, I was feeling so tired that immediately after writing a long letter to Jack, I went to bed and slept until tea time. At last, there is heating in the theatre and consequently the show went marvellously as both artists and audience were warm. Bill Marley came for us, and we again went out to the RAF mess and had a pleasant evening.

The padre was in good form and amused us with quotations from some of the letters he received. We returned to the hostel in a jeep about 1.00 am, my first ride in a jeep and I was frozen. To bed at 2.00 am. Steve took me to see his signals office –

---

[6] An RAF Padre was a military chaplain serving with the Royal Air Force, responsible for the spiritual and emotional well-being of airmen. These chaplains provided religious services, counselling, and moral support to personnel, whether on airbases, in the field, or during operations. Padres were often seen as a comforting and trusted presence, offering guidance, leading prayers, and conducting funerals for fallen comrades. They provided support regardless of faith or background. Beyond their pastoral duties, RAF Padres also helped boost morale, organised recreational activities and provided a reassuring presence in times of fear and uncertainty.

mobile[7] , and I was surprised at the comparative comfort there is in such a small vehicle. It was all very interesting.

December 29th Friday 1944

Awoke about 10.30 am, had a bath and did some washing. Went for coffee with Vivienne and after lunch, we went with Steve and Jim to hear the Halle Orchestra at Philips Hall. John Barbirolli conducted and they gave a delightful program. Apart from a little coughing in the first half, I enjoyed it immensely, particularly the Beethoven overture and the Spanish Dance by Rimsky Korsakov. When we arrived at the theatre, we found another dressing room flooded, what a theatre! Quite a good show, our friends were in the front again. Afterwards, we returned again to the mess, which is speedily becoming our second home – we look forward to going and I think we will miss it next week. Tig was in bed with a touch of laryngitis so Marjorie stayed with him all the evening. They said in all seriousness how grateful they are for our company, which has

---

[7] During World War II, Mobile Signals Offices were vital for military communication, operating from specially equipped trucks or trailers fitted with radios, teleprinters, and encryption devices. These mobile units kept commanders connected to frontline troops, relaying orders and intelligence where fixed lines were impractical or too risky. Staffed by skilled signals personnel, Mobile signal offices ensured secure, fast communication, often working under intense battlefield conditions. Some also intercepted enemy transmissions, aiding intelligence efforts. Whether supporting ground forces, coordinating air operations, or linking naval units, these mobile offices were the unseen backbone of wartime communications, keeping operations running smoothly in the chaos of war.

made them start looking to their personal appearance again after so many months of male company only. We, in our turn, have enjoyed their company enormously, so it's been a case of mutual morale lifting. Retired at about 2.00 am as usual. You have been thinking of me again this evening Jack, I know. Good night.

December 30th Saturday 1944

Arose at 10.30 am pressed my skirt, cleaned all my shoes and packed. Dull matinee after which Jimmie came and took us back to the mess for tea. The evening show was very good, I worked well because I was annoyed about the rumours going around to the effect that we shouldn't be allowed to go to the dance. After the show, Rogers gave us a lecture and said that we were not allowed to travel in transport other than that provided by ENSA, also that we had to be in by midnight! That of course put paid to the dance – the boys came for us and after we'd explained everything to them, we walked (or rather skated over the ice) to their mess, had half an hour's chat and walked back again. Betsy and Mac came too as she couldn't travel with him to Helmond. When we got back to the hostel, again we sat and talked until 2.30 am. Said goodbye to Steve, Tig and Bill and went to bed. We have heard that excellent reports of the show have gone to Brussels, so it might hasten our journey there. Plenty of 'war' going on tonight, plus fly-bombs in plenty. Tomorrow, we go even nearer to the line. Goodnight Jack.

December 31st Sunday 1944

Left Eindhoven at 1.30 pm and had a pleasant journey to Breda[8]. The hostel here is very comfortable; I am sharing with Marjorie and Freda and all the rooms have stoves. Unpacked after dinner and had a very much needed rest until supper at 8.30 pm. Mrs Pullin, the welfare officer called and gave us an invitation to a Canadian mess party. Three officers called for us. We were seven girls and we walked to their mess, which is only a few doors away. They're all very decent types and we had a most enjoyable time with them. I was with Major Murray all the evening and we had a most serious conversation all the evening, in between dancing to the radiogram, eating and drinking. We let the New Year in hilariously and as the saying goes, 'a good time was had by all' even Marion enjoyed herself! I am revising my opinion of the Canadians, the men over here are definitely picked men and from what Murray told me, they are much friendlier than the English boys, although I pointed out that that was just a matter of temperament. Murray is of Scottish descent, a mixture of Inverness and near Glasgow, and I was most entertained by his descriptions of Montreal where he lives. I certainly hope we meet them all again. Happy New Year Jack darling.

---

[8] Nestled in the southern Netherlands, the city of Breda was Liberated by Polish forces in October 1944. Breda became a crucial base for Allied operations in the region, supporting efforts to secure the Scheldt estuary and open the port of Antwerp. While specific records of ENSA performances are difficult to trace, it is documented that ENSA troupes were active in the Netherlands during this period and that some ENSA entertainers performed twice-daily concerts for troops at the front lines in an attempt to boost morale by providing a reminder of home and some brief moments of escape.

2

January 1945

January 1st Monday 1945

After a very active night in the way of gunfire, fly-bombs and Jerry reconnaissance planes plus a spot of hangover – arose for a taste of breakfast. Bet gave me a haircut and I finished a letter home and gave myself, Marj and Freda a facial. Murray came for me after lunch and we had a lovely walk all around Breda. He knows his way very well and we didn't miss a thing – even the children's fair! We returned to his mess and I drank a tankard of delicious cold beer – the very first time I've even enjoyed it. I stayed about half an hour and he saw me back to the hostel. Feeling much better after the outing, we gave quite a good show at the G.T. although there was a nasty 'tank trap[9]' Early to bed worn out! Bought two ties and some woollen gloves from the officer's shop. Hope the post comes.

January 2nd Tuesday 1945

Awakened at about 4.00 am by buzz-bombs[10] and gunfire, but I was soon asleep again, although in fact, there was great activity at close quarters all night. Went out shopping this morning and visited the officer's shop again for handkerchiefs. Had a cup of tea at the NAAFI, where a good Canadian band was playing. Stayed in all afternoon waiting for the post. Bet and I were stopped in the street by a Jewish woman who recognised us and although we couldn't say a word to her, we were all smiles. The show went very well and we had a good audience. Back to the hostel for supper and retired early to wash my hair. No

---

[9] A tank trap was an obstacle designed to slow down or stop enemy tanks and armoured vehicles, often used as part of defensive lines. In WWII, these traps came in various forms, for example, Anti-tank ditches with deep, wide trenches that tanks would get stuck in or struggle to cross. Concrete obstacles or Dragon's Teeth, with pyramid-shaped concrete blocks arranged to prevent tanks from passing. Steel beams and hedgehogs with large, X-shaped metal structures that could block roads and beaches. Mines and explosive traps with hidden explosives to destroy tanks if they drove over them.

[10] A buzz bomb was the nickname for the V-1 flying bomb, a German unmanned missile used in World War II. It got its name from the distinctive buzzing sound of its jet engine, which cut out just before impact—leaving an eerie silence before the explosion. Launched from ramps or dropped from aircraft, it could travel great distances at speed. While terrifying, the V-1 was eventually replaced by the more advanced V-2 rocket, which was faster and even harder to defend against.

post today,[11] so we were all disappointed. I hope the Canadians invite me to their mess again! Goodnight Jack.

January 3rd Wednesday 1945

As usual, we wandered out this morning, had tea at the NAAFI [12] and arrived back at the hostel for lunch. There is still no sign of any post and we are all fed up about it. I stayed in all afternoon, did jobs and had a little sleep. The show went well and we were delighted to meet our RAF padre again with letters for us from the boys at Eindhoven. He came back and had supper with us and we've arranged for the boys to come over on Sunday, all being well. I've got neuralgia in the left side of my face and I'm feeling rather homesick for J. At the moment I wish he was here now, bless him. Goodnight.

---

[11] Even on the front lines, Allied troops could still send and receive post from loved ones thanks to a well-organised military mail system. Letters were collected and sorted by the Army Postal Service, using Field Post Offices (FPOs) near battle zones and Base Post Offices for those further afield. Mail travelled by ship, convoy, or air when possible, though delays were common. Airgraphs, a system where letters were photographed and printed at their destination, helped speed up delivery. Staying connected through letters was a vital morale booster, offering soldiers a sense of normalcy, comfort, and motivation in the midst of war.

[12] The NAAFI (Navy, Army and Air Force Institutes) provided canteens, shops, and entertainment for servicemen and women. During World War II, it supplied troops with food, cigarettes, toiletries, and small comforts, even in remote or war-torn areas. Found on military bases, ships, and camps, NAAFI canteens also offered entertainment like dances and films, giving soldiers a much-needed break.

January 4th Thursday 1945

The morning was spent out as usual after another busy night. After lunch Betsy, Edna, Kay and I went to see Bing Crosby on 'Going My Way' and we all enjoyed it immensely. The ENSA transport broke down and was fixed at 7.00 pm, so the show went up late, but they were an excellent audience. We were invited to a dance afterwards by some RAF officers, but I didn't care for them at all and was glad when Morris called the roll. I do so wish the Major would call again; I would like to see him again. We still haven't received any mail and I'm missing you like hell Jack. Perhaps tomorrow! Goodnight.

January 5th Friday 1945

Another beautiful day and out for the usual constitutional, returned to the hostel to find that the mail had arrived at last. Two letters from home and two from Jack. Felt much better after that and immediately after lunch, wrote to Jack, Auntie Flo and Ruth wishing her happy birthday. Mummy's letters were full of the Xmas gatherings and Jack's full of love and sweetness, bless him. Told us that Auntie Flo had broken her arm and I bet he's looking after her like a real nurse. We were all feeling happy again and consequently gave a super show. Our Canadian friends were in front and I'm sure they all enjoyed themselves. The three 'brown jobs' were also round to apologise for their drunken behaviour last night. Bet and I both bought very attractive brooches of white enamel to take home for presents. Goodnight.

January 6th Saturday 1945

Morning constitutional after another noisy night. Bought a silver Egyptian ring and some red earrings at a little art shop. Freda gave me a very pretty brooch as a birthday present. Stayed in all afternoon and had a sleep. The evening show was very good, more of our Canadian friends were in the front row and Betsy's Peter was here for the third time. Jim has thawed out again and we are all allowed to be cheerful again! He announced that we are going to make a party next Friday for all the staff here and all our friends. I would like to ask Murray – perhaps I will. I'm very tired, so I'll read your letter again and go to sleep. Goodnight.

January 7th Sunday 1945

Ruth's birthday

Had a bad night with face ache and tummy ache so stayed in bed until lunchtime and then went down to meet padre Ward, Bill, Steve and Jamie who came over for the day. After lunch, we all went to the cinema to see Teresa Wright in 'Shades of Doubt' with Joseph Cotton. Back for tea and then the padre led us all to a very nice little pub where we drank beer till dinner time. The RAF departed after dinner. Had a pleasant day, and then we all went to an army mess dance, where we enjoyed ourselves immensely. The mess was a pre-war nightclub and a really beautiful place. A simply smashing buffet with the most delicious delicacies, sweet and savoury and lots of very good drink. I danced solidly from 10.00 pm till 1.30 am and then walked home with Lt. Alec How, he's going home to

England tomorrow on leave. Goodnight. Forgot to mention that last night we received more mail from home with little messages from the whole family and also another card from Lilley announcing her engagement. On our way back from the dance we were stopped by the MP's who were most apologetic when they saw my cap badge! The snow has settled and looks very lovely tonight and the sky is full of stars.

Rita Ernstein in ENSA uniform

January 8th Monday 1945

I awoke after a good night's rest, slightly disturbed by the noisy departure of our Canadian friends at about 7.00 am. It has been snowing hard all the morning and Bet and I went to the officer's shop to have our battle tunics altered. After lunch, I did a load of ironing and we set off early – about 4.00 pm for the GT at Tilburg. The theatre is very cosy and we are sharing a dressing room with Marjorie, the only drawback is that the electricity is not switched on till about 6.30 pm so we had to unpack by candlelight. The audience was mainly Canadian and fortunately the show went well. Just before we started, Morris came around with more mail and I had a lovely letter from Jack, which made me feel very happy. We had trouble starting the transport, but eventually, we returned to the hostel at Breda at around 11.00 pm. I'm feeling very tired tonight, in fact, I hardly had the energy to make the usual preparations for bed. However, I'm in bed now and all's well! The snow has frozen, so it will be a slippery business tomorrow. Goodnight darling and thanks for my letter.

January 9th Tuesday 1945

Stayed in bed all this morning as I am still feeling weary despite a good night's sleep. After lunch, I went for a walk with Betty, called into the officer's shop and bought ourselves leather jerkins[13] and had a cup of tea in the NAAFI whilst writing postcards to the family. We bought a few little novelties to take home, a wall plaque of a Dutch kitchen and a pair of small sabots. Early tea and off to the show at Tilburg[14]. We have transferred the show to the big theatre as they have had to turn hundreds of men away every night up to date. Sounds good but it's been an awful nuisance. Heard today that we will be in Holland another week and shall be going somewhere north of Eindhoven. The snow has frozen hard and seems to have come to stay. Very tired, Good night.

January 10th Wednesday 1945

Had a peaceful night and slept like a log. Arose about 10.00am and set Freda's hair and was busy all the morning altering the black jacket for our act, it feels most uncomfortable as it is. Travelled by truck to the 88th General Hospital where we put

---

[13] Leather jerkins were sleeveless, thick leather coats worn over uniforms for warmth and protection. Issued to British and Commonwealth troops in World War II, they provided insulation while allowing free movement, making them ideal for soldiers in cold, wet conditions. Typically brown leather with a wool lining, they buttoned down the front and were widely used by infantry, tank crews, and engineers. Some ENSA performers also wore them while touring with the troops, offering warmth during travel and outdoor performances in harsh wartime environments.

[14] By January 1945, Tilburg, a city in the South of the Netherlands, had become a key Allied base following its liberation in October 1944. The city served as a staging area for troops preparing for Operation Veritable, a major offensive aimed at breaking through German defences. British soldiers stationed in Tilburg helped manage liberated areas.

on one hours show for the boys. They did appreciate it and afterwards we had tea with the nurses and doctors. At about 5.30 pm we left and went straight to the cinema which we have taken over for the rest of the week. The audience was terrific and I really enjoyed the rest of the show. Back to Breda in the same truck, absolutely up to our eyes in clothing but quite warm. Supper, washed and bed. Thank goodness I'm feeling better and less weary. Goodnight. Must write to Jack tomorrow! Mona had ten teeth out today.

January 11th Thursday 1945

Had a very busy morning, washed my hair, altered finally my black jacket, ironed and then cleaned shoes. Felt very sleepy after lunch so had forty winks and then wrote to Jack. The Eindhoven crowd came backstage during the show and we made arrangements to have lunch at the mess on Sunday on our way to Hasselt in Belgium[15] where we are working next week. After the show we returned to the mess and had a very pleasant evening with our friends of last Sunday. I danced until I thought my legs would buckle under me, I was so utterly tired.

---

[15] By January 1945, Hasselt, Belgium, was no longer on the front battle lines but remained important to the Allied war effort. Since its liberation in September 1944, the city had become a logistical hub, helping to supply and support troops as they prepared for the final push into Germany. Its roads and railways were vital for moving soldiers, equipment, and supplies, making it a key link in the Allies' operations. The city was also used for storing and distributing large amounts of petroleum, and oil for the military.

For the first time in my life I had oysters and champagne and loved 'em! Morris gave us one of his managerial lectures tonight and as usual all the complaints were directed at us girls – it's always safe to blame the girls! Goodnight darling I've missed you very much tonight.

January 12th Friday 1945

Disturbed at about 8.00 am by a terrific explosion which shook the house – the return of the V-2s. Went for a walk before lunch, called in at the NAAFI and wrote to mummy over a cup of tea. Back to lunch in the snow and then did a spot of packing, after which I was compelled to have a nap. The necessity for afternoon sleep is getting serious! Something about burning the candle at both ends!! Another good show and then back to the hostel to entertain the people that Jim invited over. Afraid I've sadly neglected my duties and popped up to bed early, feeling absolutely worn out. I'll probably get a lecture from Betty in the morning. Goodnight love.

January 13th Saturday 1945

Went for a walk as far as the officer's shop and was surprised to find the padre at the hostel for lunch. We had an early call before which I did a spot of packing. The padre and George came to the show at Tilburg in the evening and arranged for an escort to Eindhoven for lunch tomorrow. After the show we were invited to a Canadian mess, and Kay, Edna and I went and spent a very pleasant evening. Strangely enough, all these boys know Yorkshire and one in particular is of Yorkshire parentage. We were escorted back to the hostel and eventually rolled into bed about 3.00 am. Had a dreadful night's sleep and feeling very sick. There was also constant artillery fire in the distance.

January 14th Sunday 1945

Arose about 9.00 am feeling very sick and could not face any breakfast. At 10.30am we left Breda in an open truck, each one of us laden with clothing and hugging hot water bottles. The padre met us on the way and led us to the mess at Eindhoven, where we had an excellent lunch – I couldn't eat anything! Meanwhile, Jim and Morris had words at the hostel with the welfare officer, and it was eventually arranged that the RAF would transport us to Hasselt, as we refused to travel further in the truck.

The first load left at 3.30 pm and I spent the afternoon on Steve's bed resting. Came down to tea and spent the rest of the time with Steve in his mobile office. The padre returned at about 8.30 pm and at 9.30 pm we set out again with Steve and Bill and arrived safely at the hostel in Hasselt. Made tea for the boys and arranged a party for them next Friday, all being well. They have been so kind to us and it was a real pleasure to return to their mess to meet Tig and the rest of their colleagues. I gave Victor my Egyptian ring to give to his wife and he was very pleased with it. It's now nearly 2.00 am and I'm all in. Thank goodness this is a more comfortable bed than the one I've had for the past two weeks. Goodnight.

January 15th Monday 1945

I stayed in bed all morning as I was feeling none too good and arose at lunchtime and had a bath (the first blessed bath for a fortnight) and then went to the restaurant where we have our meals. After my lunch (a plate of soup) I returned to the hostel and spent the afternoon in bed, getting up again to go out to tea. We called at the office to change some of our gilders to francs and picked up our mail: two letters from home and one from Auntie Flo. The theatre is next door to the hostel and is very old indeed and cold! The stage consists mainly of a series of trap doors and large metal hinges and is impossible for dancing. Our dressing room has a most peculiar stove which however provides the necessary heat and the walls are covered with ancient photos of pro's. The show went very well, although the audience must have been petrified. I returned to the hostel and bed as I couldn't face supper. Goodnight.

January 16th Tuesday 1945

Arose at 10.00 am feeling fine. Skipped breakfast and did a complete tour of inspection of Hasselt with Bett. It's a beautiful day, sunshine and ice and the shops are crammed full of everything. After lunch, we took Morris with us to the photographers as interpreter and had two sittings each, with and without our service caps. We then enjoyed ourselves thoroughly buying perfume – Worth, and Bet bought me a Worth lipstick with two refills as a birthday present. She bought some Dana perfume, also French and we have seen some superb jewellery that we are thinking of buying Mummy on payday.

We have cleaned ourselves out today! Whilst shopping we saw General Montgomery pass in his car and there is a suspicion that he may see the show. We had a packed house tonight and the boxes were full of officers – they always wait for Monday's report! After the show, I skipped supper and did my washing. I don't suppose for one moment that I will lose any weight by skipping meals. Wrote to Mummy. Have enjoyed today thoroughly despite the fact and probably because I'm skint. Might hear from Jack tomorrow. Goodnight.

January 17th Wednesday 1945

Arose about 10.00 am after another disturbed night feeling too weak for words. Managed to get myself ready for lunch. We had a matinee today and I really don't know how I got through it. No letter from Jack, I'm disappointed however, perhaps tomorrow! Had a sleep between shows and felt much better we had a smashing audience and I've worked with more energy than I've been able to muster all week. Didn't want any supper so made myself some coffee, had a bath and I'm now in bed. I do hope I feel myself tomorrow as I'm not used to feeling off colour. Please let me hear from you tomorrow. Goodnight my love.

January 18th Thursday 1945

Stayed in all morning and did jobs. After lunch, had an early pick up for a hospital show. We played the hospital where Joe is an in-patient and they were a good audience, stayed there for tea and then walked to the office and collected the long-awaited parcel from home. Immediately wrote to Mummy acknowledging its receipt and by that time we were due at the theatre. Had a spot of excitement when quite a number of brass hats from SHAEF[16] turned up in the dress circle but we haven't yet discerned exactly who they were. Gave an excellent show and went back for supper for the first time this week. The ghost walked and I did a spot of exchange with Miss Dow for Belgium francs. Jim is ignoring me after the tiff this afternoon at the hospital. Some on that later maybe! I shall have to have it all out with him. Still no letter from Jack, I'm so longing for one. Good night.

January 19th Friday 1945

Set Freda's hair and then went out with Bet and had a lovely time buying outrageously expensive stockings and nail varnish. Stayed in after lunch, called at the office, changed some money and had a chat with the sergeant in charge. Steve, Bill, Victor, Jimmie, Tig and Bob came from Eindhoven and occupied a box at the theatre. We were again honoured with important patrons but still no sign of Monty and we were all a bit disappointed.

---

[16] SHAEF (Supreme Headquarters Allied Expeditionary Force)was the high command of Allied forces in Western Europe, led by General Dwight D. Eisenhower. It was responsible for planning and overseeing the Allied invasion of Europe, including D-Day (June 6, 1944) and the subsequent campaign to defeat Nazi Germany. SHAEF coordinated military operations between American, British, Canadian, and other Allied forces, ensuring effective strategy, logistics, and communication. It was officially formed in December 1943 and played a crucial role until the end of the war in Europe in May 1945.

After supper we had a very pleasant evening in the hostel and fortunately, our spirit ration[17] had arrived which, together with the stuff the boys brought helped things considerably. Steve also brought my bracelet and I love it! He goes home on leave tomorrow and I shan't see him again, I like him a lot, it's been a good month. They departed at about 3.00 am and when seeing them to their car, we found the snow thick and the stars bright, in fact the town looked just like a picture post card. Forgot to mention that the corporal at the theatre who has mended my taps comes from Hawthorn Ave!!! Received letters from home and Edgeware in which we learned that the buzz bombs have found Hull. Kay also learned that her home in London had been demolished. Still no news from Jack – terribly disappointed. Goodnight.

January 20th Saturday 1945

Arose early at 9.30 am and washed my hair. Lovely morning so Bet and I again made our way to the perfume shop and enjoyed ourselves spending more francs. Arrived at the theatre and put on my makeup for the matinee but at 2.40 pm it was cancelled, not enough audience! All greatly relieved so spent the afternoon

---

[17] During World War II, ENSA performers were often entitled to a spirit ration, a government issued allowance of alcohol. Their spirit ration typically included whiskey, rum, or gin, similar to what was issued to British soldiers, although it was not guaranteed. It is believed that the allowance was also given to help ENSA entertainers integrate with the military personnel they performed for, as shared drinks were a common way to bond and unwind after performances. Though not as strictly regulated as military rations, ENSA's alcohol supply was still controlled, particularly in more active war zones where resources were scarce.

packing and sleeping. Evening show went well but the audience was distinctly dull. Afterwards had lots of photographs taken by a couple of RAF blokes. One of them has promised to send some home for us when he goes on leave. On our way home from supper we had a lovely snow fight with Edna, Betty, Alan and Pt. Alec Furnell, we enjoyed ourselves like kids. To bed about 12.30 am. Goodnight.

January 21st Sunday 1945

Waited two hours for the transport and eventually set off from Hasselt at 12.30 pm. Beautiful sunny day and everything all the way was covered thickly with snow, making the otherwise demolished houses, broken roads and ammo dumps, look less gruesome and more part of the whole lovely picture. We passed wooded country and lovely houses and everything sparkled and shone in the sunlight. Arrived at Hasselt at 2.00 pm and had lunch at the pub where all the girls are staying. There is no heating whatsoever here and there's a 5.30 pm curfew. One of the streets is named 'Enemy Ahead' which makes me begin to realise that we are very near the fun at last! After lunch, I wrote to Jack and also a few postcards to various acquaintances. In the evening we sat and spent the whole time reading and writing in the public saloon, the only warm room in the house. We were both surprised to meet Col Bentley's brother Jim, who is a sergeant on the ack-ack[18] and we had a long chat with him. He is going home on leave on Friday and has promised to phone home and talk to Mummy: she will be surprised! Retired about 11.30 pm to our freezing bedroom and got 'dressed' for the night. Naturally, there has been plenty of gunfire all night. Must try and wangle a spot of fuel for the stove tomorrow, we have added to the meagre lighting of the room by putting a few candles in the ostentatious but shabby candelabra.

January 22nd Monday 1945

After a hellish night – or rather, I should say a frozen night we arose at 9.30 am and queued up for hot water. That successfully obtained, had a very quick wash, and by the time I was fully dressed, I could neither feel my fingers nor my feet. Gave this minute town the once over and was glad to return to the warm saloon to thaw out. The air is positively cutting, my eyes were watering and I felt as if I were walking on my knees. Early lunch and then the journey to the show. It was a very interesting drive, everything white with snow, of course. We passed over the river Maas by a very fragile looking army bridge and then over the Juliana Canal in Holland. We knew we were in Holland by the two windmills in action! We arrived very late and rang up at 3.15 pm. The audience was good and the conditions are excellent – plus heat. Afterwards, had tea with officers who

---

[18] "Ack Ack" was military slang for anti-aircraft guns used to defend against enemy aircraft in World War II. These guns were vital in protecting cities, airfields, and military bases. Ack Ack crews used radar, searchlights, and sound locators to track enemy planes, firing shells that exploded mid-air, and spraying deadly shrapnel.

tried to persuade us to dance but we were all in battledress and boots and had the long journey back, so we refused. Spent the evening in the saloon talking to Tom the Scotty, who has promised us some coal. Went to bed in pyjamas, dressing gown and socks and was fairly warm. Waiting for mail again. The theatre is at Hoensbruek.

January 23rd Tuesday 1945

Awakened at 8.30 am by a terrific din going on in the street below our window. Had to satisfy my curiosity and found the cause of the racket to be truck loads of Belgian workmen waiting to be transported somewhere or other! Hopped back into bed again and eventually hiked down for hot water at 9.30 am. Stayed in all morning and set out for Hoensbruek[19] after an early lunch. Dull matinee but a good evening show after which we had light refreshments and started the return journey.

After a few miles, we lost the escorting lorry in which Vivienne was sitting beside the driver, Terry. We eventually found ourselves no more than 4000 yards from the front line and the gunfire was terrific. We made several stops to find our way to the right side of the river and after travelling for the best part of three hours, we arrived safely at Maaseik to find no

---

[19] Hoensbroek is in the South East of the Netherlands, close to the German border. about 14 miles from Maaseik. Maaseik is a town in Belgium, near the Dutch border along the Meuse River (Maas River).

Vivienne. We are all terribly worried because Terry turned off[20] the enemy lines. We stayed up very late, hoping they would return, but eventually, we had to go to bed.

January 24th Wednesday 1945

Awoke early and went immediately to the girls' room to see if Vivienne had returned – she hadn't. At 11.30 am Miss Dow and Cpt de Wolf arrived and we knew things were serious, they told us the news. The truck hit a mine, Terry is injured and Vivienne is dead! We are all terribly upset naturally. Vivienne Fayre (real name Hole) was the baby of the company at only 19. I can't help thinking that but for the grace of God, it might have been us all. It's so hard to realise that we shan't see her mischievous little smile again. I didn't think I could grow so fond of a person in such a short time. We decided to do the show as usual, but we were all thankful when it was over. Tom, our Scotty friend, took Bet, Edna and I to his cookhouse for supper and he did his best to cheer us up. He managed to get us a sack of coal, so we returned to find a beautiful fire in our room and we were very grateful for the comfort. The funeral is

---

[20] The phrase "turned off" might refer to the vehicle turning off the route and becoming separated from the rest of the convoy, or it could imply shutting down or losing a radio connection. Research suggests that Vivienne Hole was the only active ENSA member to be killed during World War II. The same sources state that her truck, carrying the scenery for the stage show, accidentally entered a minefield. She died en route to the field hospital. However, a comment in Rita's entry on Sunday, February 4th 1945 may suggest the reported story changed some of the information, as was common at the time, to protect military intelligence. Some sources during my research suggest the incident happened in Normandy.

to be held tomorrow and we have had the two shows cancelled. This dreadful day is over at last. I hate this place and dread the journeys back from the theatre. Goodnight.

Vivienne Inez Hole (1925 - 1945)

January 25th Thursday 1945

Came down to breakfast – real eggs! After which I cleaned out the stove and made a good fire, tidied the bedroom and did my washing. The funeral took place at 3.00 pm at Sittard military cemetery, Ophoven, Netherlands. There were three wreaths from Joe, Rhymes & Rhythm and Col. Hogarth. The ceremony was simple, officiated by the chief Chaplain and the last post was sounded. We were all brave and drip-eyed until the last post and I'm afraid we all broke down then. Many other Scottish soldiers from the Maintain Regiment were also being buried in graves, dug by German prisoners, but they didn't have officers and we could see their boots sticking out of the blankets! The graves were all covered in snow and I was disgusted to see so many native onlookers. I never dreamt that the first funeral I attended would be under such tragic circumstances and in such a place. We returned for tea and played cards with Tom and Tig until supper, afterwards we went with Capt. Foster (a Hull-ite) and Lt. Lamb to their office where we sat, talked and drank for a while. Two letters from home and one from Jack were waiting for us and cheered me up no end. Harold is expected home (from India) in about a month's time – I can understand how happy Sylvia must be. Goodnight and thank you.

January 26th Friday 1945

Stayed in all the morning and set off at about 12.30 pm for the theatre, minus Betsy (who has to stay in bed for a few days because of a strained heart and general low condition), Freda and Jack who are both ill. We gave two shows and considering all the gaps and makeshifts, the shows were excellent. Capt. Skinner and the Major were taking photographs throughout the show and were enjoying themselves immensely. Capt. Skinner gave me a pair of minute wooden clogs made by one of the men which I am keeping for auntie Flo. After supper on our return I wrote to Jack, a difficult job amid the turmoil of the saloon. Morris informed us that we are returning to Hasselt next week and there is general rejoicing at the news. Just before we retired, Bet took up the water bottles and discovered a drunken officer fast asleep in our bed! She dashed into the saloon looking as though she had seen a ghost and some of the boys had to drag him out and dress him. Really this place is the limit – it only needs a red light outside! The fire in our room is a comfort and we have done all our writing and washing to save us from doing it in the freezing cold in the morning. And so to bed. Goodnight.

January 27th Saturday 1945

Early pick up at 11.30 am so that we could have lunch in the mess before the show. We did one show only and the audience was rather dull, Freda was back again – her old self! We were delighted to see Victor, who had come from Eindhoven specially to see us and we took him to tea, then received Mrs Cox's permission to drive back with him and George to Maaseik. Before we left Hoensbruek, an army M.T. office caught fire and Don just saved our coach from catching fire by dashing into the driver's seat and getting it out of the vicinity. The fire was quickly under control, but Bill and Peter, two of the officers, were badly burned and had to be taken to hospital. Both had face injuries and looked pretty ghastly. We bid a hasty farewell to Capt. Tom Skinner and set out. Halfway back, the convoy stopped and we learned that Marjorie, having recovered from a dead faint, was having hysterics! A grand finale to a week of tragedy and mishaps. We arrived safely at the billet, Victor and George stayed for supper, visited the invalids and sold us some lovely D'Orsay perfume, which he had brought specially for us – he's an angel and we are both very fond of him. They left about 11.00 pm and we returned to finish packing. I hope we never see this dreadful place again! Goodnight.

January 28th Sunday 1945

Coach call at 10.30 am, which meant the usual half hours delay, we eventually set out after 11.00 am after saying goodbye to our Scottish friend Tom. Travelled through As and Genk[21] and arrived at the Hasselt hostel at about 12.30 pm and we met the Rhyme and Rhythm Co. before they left to Maaseik. We all had lunch together in the dining room and received quite a bumper mail. Letters from Mummy, Auntie Flo, Freda, Phyllis and Michael. Unpacked and spent the afternoon writing. Feeling rather depressed at the moment as Auntie Flo's letter has upset me, however, I'm glad to be back here in a comfortable,

---

[21] 'As' and 'Genk' are two towns in Northeastern Belgium. This region of Limburg saw significant activity during WWII. Asch Airfield near Genk, was constructed by the U.S. Army Air Forces in November 1944 and was the site of a major aerial battle in January 1945.

warm bedroom; at the moment, I'm sitting by the window in the lounge, overlooking the square where children are having a great time snowballing. Joe returned from hospital this afternoon. His face has healed very well, but he's lost a lot of weight and the leg that has taken infection is very painful. He can't walk properly yet however he's very glad to be back with us again. A Belgium party arrived at tea time, 16 of 'em and George wasn't warned! Continued writing and reading until supper. The doctor came to see Marj and said she must stay in bed a few days, so we'll be having an enforced holiday. She's suffering from shock and knowing Marjorie, she won't make the effort to recover! Retired at 10.30 pm to our lovely bed. Goodnight.

January 29th Monday 1945

Betty has been ill all night, and I'm afraid she's got the Hasselt complaint. Before lunch, Edna and I did a spot of shopping, nail varnish, sweets and apples and then called for our photos, which are very good. When we returned, we found Capt. Bill and his C.O. and Major Brown, REME[22] awaiting us. They had come to investigate about the fire accident, they stayed for lunch and we learned from Bill, who had just been discharged from the hospital, that Peter was in the 81st hospital here. After lunch, Kay, Freda and I went to see Peter. His head is a sight

---

[22] REME stands for the Royal Electrical and Mechanical Engineers, a corps of the British Army responsible for repairing and maintaining military equipment. Established in October 1942, REME ensured that tanks, trucks, weapons, radios, and other essential equipment remained operational on the battlefield.

and his hands are bandaged. I spent a dreadful hour with him feeling very sick and faint and wishing the time would pass quickly. I'm afraid I made a very feeble effort at cheerfulness, but he was delighted to see us. When we arrived, there was a stack of mail waiting for me, an airgraph[23] from Ron, a letter from Sylvia, Nita, Mummy and Jack. Mummy and Jack's letters were full of mutual admiration, but again I shed a few tears – I wish I could stop worrying. After tea, the healthy members of the Co., including myself, saw the Belgian show and I enjoyed every minute of it. I would never have thought that tatty, untidy looking mob could have possessed such talent and personality – it just goes to show! Mona introduced us to Mai Bacon at supper – she arrived by plane this afternoon. I beat Kay at rummy and retired; I hope Bet feels better tomorrow. Goodnight, dearest and thanks for your letter. Annette's birthday today.

January 30th Tuesday 1945

I have stayed in all day and although I have filled the time in well enough, I've been slightly bored the whole time. First of all, I had to wait until 12.00 o'clock to wash my hair as the water was barely lukewarm. Then, I did a spot of ironing with the borrowed iron, for which I was extremely grateful. This afternoon I finished reading 'Private Gollantz' by Naomi

---

[23] An airgraph was a microfilmed letter used by British and Allied forces during World War II to speed up postal communication. Instead of transporting full letters, the message was photographed onto microfilm, sent by air, and then printed and delivered at its destination. This system saved space on military aircraft while ensuring letters could still reach soldiers and loved ones quickly.

Jacobs, had a lukewarm bath and cleaned myself up generally. The M.O[24] arrived after tea and pronounced none of the invalids ready for work until Thursday at least. Betty has also succumbed and her complaint (sickness, tummy ache and diarrhoea) is infectious – it would be! For want of anything better to do, I made the patients a huge jug of lemon water, then wrote a long letter to Jack and sent him my 'glamorous' photos. I have written innumerable letters during the past two days and I'm fed up. The boredom of tomorrow looms interminably ahead. We are now waiting for supper time and after that I shall probably retire so I'll say goodnight now.

January 31st Wednesday 1945

Went shopping with Kay and Freda and bought a tiny bottle of Chanel perfume and a pair of white flower earrings. Spent the afternoon sitting with Betty and visiting all the patients. Fell asleep at the bottom of the bed out of sheer boredom. After the M.O. had passed Bet as fit to eat (great rejoicing on her part), she washed her hair and I set it. I took supper up to all the invalids and tired myself out running up and down the stairs. Had a delicious hot bath and played rummy with Kay and after three games I won 5 pence! I retired early feeling even more weary than if I'd done three shows. The thaw is making everything very messy. Goodnight.

---

[24] An MO (Medical Officer) in the military is a doctor responsible for the health and well-being of military personnel, in WWII, this also included looking after the ENSA troupes. They provided basic medical care, vaccinations, and emergency treatment

3

February 1945

February 1st Thursday 1945

Betty got up this morning for breakfast. We went to the theatre and did the unpacking, after which we had a walk around the town. Met the charming American officer who enquired after all the patients and hoped we should be able to go over to the mess one evening. I hope so too! The major from Hoensbroek came over and stayed for lunch. Betty went with the girls to the hospital to see Peter, and I went for a walk with Sid, bought a game for Michael and an English book for myself. A simply beautiful, mild spring day so suddenly after all the snow. It was good to be working again although Edna was the only one who had to stay in bed. The house was packed and the show went very well. Retired immediately after supper - we were both very tired. Goodnight.

February 2nd Friday 1945

Another lovely day, spent more time in the bazaar on our morning outing – this time on kiddies underwear to take home to Michael and Phyl and parcelled up the game I bought for him. Went to the theatre early to rehearse the polka – I'm taking Edna's place until she's well. I had to wear Betty's dress as Edna's was too small for me. Kay achieved a miracle and got me fastened into it, but the difficulty was getting out of it! A very good audience again and I got through the polka alright. The MO was in front and enjoyed it immensely. During the show, the mail came and I had a letter from Jack and Auntie Flo. I think maybe everything will turn out alright. After the show, we went with an army officer to his mess and spent a very pleasant couple of hours. The 'misery contingent' of the company did its best to prevent us all from going, but fortunately in vain! If anyone mentions 'team spirit' to me again, I'll spit at 'em. Goodnight darling.

February 3rd Saturday 1945

Betty went to the hospital to see Peter and I did a bit of shopping for the journey. I went to the same little shop for apples and sweets and had quite a chat in French and English with the proprietor. We had a matinee but the audience was small owing to the beautiful spring sunshine outside no doubt. Victor, Bob and Bill came to tea, brought two cases of beer for the boys and saw the show again – for about the sixth time! After supper, we sat in the lounge talking until 1.00 am. Victor told us of his life as an engineer person and newspaper editor and of his future ambitions. He is very communicative and, in discussions with Miss Dow, made mincemeat of her unconvincing arguments. What an interesting life he has had so far, what infinite energy and interest in humanity he possesses! We also heard from two of the Belgium party, their experiences in occupied Belgium and France and they made us realise the great jubilation of these countries when liberated. They are both young men and they have obviously suffered. It's now 2.10 am and I shall never get up in the morning! so goodnight and God bless.

February 4th Sunday 1945

Set out at 10.30 am in the pouring rain – only one and a half hours late! Calida, a halt at Brussels where we had an excellent lunch at the hostel and picked up some mail. We received a hasty note from Stan Willis-Croft and were surprised to note that he is in Brussels. I scribbled a line to him and left it with the sergeant to be taken to the office. I hope Stan collects it. Arrived at Ghent at 4.00 pm and the hostel is perfect. The house belongs to a collaborator who is now in prison. We had another excellent meal, waited on by a sweet elderly waiter and spent the whole evening writing letters – mainly answering Jack's and Auntie Flo's. When we arrived here, there were more letters for us from Jack, Mummy and Miss Sheppard. Jack and Auntie Flo were terribly upset about Vivienne and I felt rather guilty for worrying them, in any case, they would see her photo and the 'alleged' story in yesterday's Daily Express. We saw it whilst at Brussels today. Betsy, Betty, Kay and I are sharing a room. Edna was too ill to manage the journey and we had to leave her behind at Hasselt – she is going into hospital for observation. I think we are going to have a good week here, the theatre is supposed to be perfect and there is also an eleven-piece orchestra at our disposal. Ghent appears to be an interesting place and I'm afraid I'm going to do some more spending! Goodnight, God bless.

February 5th Monday 1945

Freda's birthday – tomorrow not today! I've enjoyed every minute of the day. This morning we went to the theatre and unpacked; what a theatre! The auditorium has five balconies and there is the most beautiful chandelier, the stage is vast and the drapes are the last word. We have a dressing room of our own with hot and cold water, a wardrobe mistress and a green room for ironing. What else could we desire? Betty, Kay, Betsy and I managed to wander down one street window gazing. The shops are marvellous and the stuff costs the earth. We went into a café and payed 25 francs each for a coffee. After lunch we all went with Morris, Mona and Jack to the races and thoroughly enjoyed ourselves, up to the knees in mud but very cheerful. Besides flat races, there were trotting races and the very first race, I backed the winner! After the race my knees were weak from suspense and excitement. I won on three races out of five, and there was the funniest tall policemen who kept whispering with the jockeys, then coming back and giving us inside information, we were all amused at the bare faced cheating that was going on. The show was a great success, the orchestra was very good considering half of them had no music and I was really thrilled to be on such a magnificent stage. The audience was excellent and I saw someone taking photos during the show. This has really been a red-letter day, despite the rain and I wish Jack could have been here to share it with me. We heard from Morris today that we are going to Ostend next week. Goodnight

February 6th Tuesday 1945

Freda's birthday. We went to the theatre and I watched the orchestra rehearse, then washed and set my hair. Went with the girls and bought a little present for Freda, stayed in all the afternoon and enjoyed reading. When we arrived back at the theatre we found Colin waiting for Freda. Morris arranged a beautiful set for the polka and a log cabin effect for the hill-billy routine – both most effective. No mail today for us, retired about midnight. Goodnight.

February 7th Wednesday 1945

This morning we went shop-gazing again, there are loads of very beautiful things here in equally beautiful shops but the prices are outrageous and far beyond our means. Stayed in all afternoon. After the show, we were invited to a RAF club next door by a friend of Jim's. We started with gin and orange and we proceeded with champagne and advocaat with cherry brandy. I managed to walk steadily to the transport and a few of us who had promised, stopped off at a pub where I pretended to toy with another liqueur. We arrived back at the hostel and we were all very tight, including Jim, and then I was sick and sick and sick! I eventually fell asleep at about 2.00 am miserably cold, wretched and very ashamed of myself, as well as repentant. I vow I shall never mix my drinks again.

February 8th Thursday 1945

Awoke with a slight hangover. Went out with Betty into the town and bought some underwear at Rousells. Stayed in after lunch and gave myself a facial, then had a rest on the bed until teatime. Betty went out with Betsy and Allan and found a lovely café for tea. My handbag arrived from Maasseik today, thank goodness. The padre and George turned up at the theatre for a few minutes to say farewell – we might not see them again. Another good show, with the house filled to capacity. Retired immediately after supper and am writing this whilst waiting for Betsy to come in. She and Marj were invited out today. Goodnight and God bless.

February 9th Friday 1945

Went out for a coffee with Betty and Betsy, called in at the theatre and did a spot of washing. After lunch, we went out again and bought a swansdown puff and a lovely gilt metalbox with powder, also a tie for Daddy. Then Betsy and I went to our favourite café and had delicious pastries and lukewarm tea. These people simply can't make a hot cup of tea! Another good show. This morning, I also called into the best shoe shop in town and enquired the price of some black leather and suede wedge shoes. The cheapest were 3000 francs! Betsy and Kay are out tonight and have not yet returned. I hope they are not too late as it's 12.30 pm now. Goodnight, there may be some mail tomorrow.

February 10th Saturday 1945

Stayed in all the morning and at about 11.30 am in walks Edna, we were all delighted to have her back. After lunch, we took Ed' into the theatre and to our special café for ices and tea. She sat in a solitary state in a box during the show and enjoyed it all thoroughly. Afterwards we all went to Allan's birthday party at the little pub and had a pleasant evening. Ted produced a lovely birthday cake made by Ken (who is an army cook and comes from Doncaster) I had quite a long talk with Roger, trying to pump him on the subject of black market, but in vain! It's impossible to get anything out of these people. I don't trust any of them and I bet they're all collaborationists! We had good news today, from here we work Ostend, Bruges, Brussels and HOME!!

February 11th Sunday 1945

I was feeling lazy so skipped breakfast and stayed in bed until 10.30 am, then finished packing, whilst Bet rushed out to keep an appointment with Leon, the trumpeter. During lunch the

Phil Green[25] band arrived and we had an amusing half hour with some of the boys. We set off at 2.30 pm with the 'Good Music Co.' and arrived at Ostend at 4.15 pm. They are on their way back to England – lucky people. At about 8.30 pm Allan, Betty, Betsy and I with Marjorie, went to the Allied Club. Allan became a member and we all had a lovely time. It is a charming place and the band is excellent, although the boys look as though they are dying of consumption. We returned to the hotel at midnight, like a lot of Cinderellas, and then to bed soon after. Our room is so small that there is no room for our cases and we have to step over the beds to get to the wash basin. Goodnight darling, I hope there is some mail soon.

February 12th Monday 1945

Arose for breakfast and went to the theatre to unpack. Another lovely theatre, somewhat smaller than the opera house at Ghent. A better stage and very nice dressing rooms. Allan, Joe, Bet and I then found our way to the officer's club and had a coffee there. The devastation here is terrific and I'm finding it difficult to get the hang of this place. I had just finished writing to Jack when a bumper mail arrived for us. All the letters from home were full of Vivienne and we had two more cuttings sent to us.

---

[25] Phil Green was a British composer, conductor, and pianist. He and his band (often referred to in these memoirs as 'his boys') played a key role in entertaining Allied troops during World War II as part of ENSA. He worked with stars like Joyce Grenfell (also an ENSA performer) and provided the music for popular radio shows, including the Ovaltine broadcasts. His career extended into studio recordings, where he worked with bands and vocalists such as Joe Paradise and Marjorie Stedeford.

We had a most amusing letter from mummy with a photo of herself, which is dreadful, we sat on our beds reading all the mail aloud. After that, we spent the whole afternoon answering them. The show was simply grand, made so of course by the enthusiastic audience and I really enjoyed working on the easy stage. Allan, acting as escort, took us to the club and we had a really lovely time in company with the navy. It wasn't so crowded tonight and therefore more enjoyable for dancing. Our two naval companions were most entertaining and they eventually set us back to Ciro's at 2.00 am. The end of a perfect day. Goodnight.

February 13th Tuesday 1945

We arose about 10.30 am and kept our appointment for coffee at the officer's club with the Navy. Fred Moss, a cockney, kept us laughing all the morning, he's being sent out east any day now! This afternoon we all went to the Garrison cinema 'Laura' with Gene Tierney and Dana Andrews – it was very good. I had a little rest this evening before the show as I was feeling very tired. We had a packed house tonight and afterwards heard some good reports about the Allied Club. I was in two minds whether to go as I was so very tired, but Allan who persuaded me and Bet and so we had another party with the Navy. Tony was also there and made up the numbers, including other naval types whose names I still don't know. We packed up about 1.30 am and I was in bed at about 1.45 am. I was very homesick for Jack this evening and all the time, at the back of my mind, was the wish that he was here too. Well, it won't be long now. Goodnight.

February 14th Wednesday 1945

St. Valentine's Day, mummy and dad's wedding anniversary and a beautiful spring day. I awoke with the sun shining on my bed (about 10.00 am) to the accompaniment of Bet's ablutions! We kept our date with the Navy for coffee at the officer's club and said goodbye to Fred who was leaving for home before going out East. After lunch, we bathed and I relaxed on the bed for about half an hour. Just as I was dosing, I was rudely awakened by a terrific explosion followed by a number of smaller ones. On looking out of the window, I saw huge clouds of smoke and, on tearing downstairs, learned that an ammo boat had caught fire and the four MTBs[26] attached to it were exploding in turn with their torpedoes. Many lives have been lost and a great deal of damage caused, not only on the docks but to the little establishments in the vicinity. All the time, the army fire service and ambulances were rushing to the job. Our RAF have been

---

[26] MTB stands for Motor Torpedo Boat. These were small, fast attack boats. Armed with torpedoes, machine guns, and depth charges, they were designed for hit-and-run missions, attacking enemy convoys, patrol boats, and submarines in coastal waters. The event witnessed by Rita in Ostend on 14th February 1945 was a catastrophic fire and explosion in the harbour. It resulted in the loss of twelve Motor Torpedo Boats (MTBs) and a great number of sailors. According to the Royal Canadian Navy and Overseas Operations (1939-1945) 'Stepping Forward and Upward' *In December, the 29th Flotilla was glad when it was transferred to the liberated port of Ostend as it meant less transit time in the Channel. On Valentine's Day 1945, however, Lt. Commander Law's command met an untimely end when an accident in the crowded harbour led to the destruction by fire of 12 MTBs and the deaths of 64 officers and sailors, including 29 Canadians. As only four very worn, Canadian MTBs survived the disaster, it was decided to disband the 29th Flotilla. It was replaced at Ostend by the 65th Flotilla, which served there until the end of the war.*

going over in their thousands to Germany and now at 12.30 pm, they are still going over incessantly.

We had the usual first audience again tonight and after supper, we retired early to bed. I was surprised on going into Freda's dressing room tonight to find Collin there. He's just popped over for the night. It's been a most enjoyable day apart from the excitement – we literally never have a dull moment in this company. Sid heard by wire today of the death of his father at the age of 92 and is going home tomorrow on compassionate leave. Goodnight.

February 15th Thursday 1945

Washed my hair and coffee'd with Allan and Kay at the officer's club, after which we had a walk down to the docks but could see little owing to the mist. Ostend is in a state of almost complete devastation and what was once the casino is now a ruin, in front of which is a fortress–like erection built by the Germans as a lookout. We met Bonny and Tony for afternoon tea and were glad to learn that none of their crowd were in yesterday's trouble. After the show, we were taken to Navy House as guests and met Commander Patrick. He is a very quiet little man but rather charming and of course we were talking with Mrs Pat and Sheila. The dance finished at midnight and we all made our way to the Allied Club, where Allan managed to get us all in and we danced until 2.00 am when we decided it was time for some sleep. Allan had the key so all went well and we eventually turned out the lights at 2.30 am. Goodnight.

February 16th Friday 1945

Arose, bid farewell to Sid, who is going home by plane today and met the Navy again for coffee. Had tea with the two mates, Brenda and Megan and we were joined by Bonny. They all came to see the show and when we met them at the club afterwards, they told us how much they'd enjoyed it. We received some mail from home and the shirt that Jack sent me arrived – it's a beauty! We didn't stay very long at the club as we were all very tired. Returned at 01.00 am. Goodnight and thanks.

February 17th Saturday 1945

Betty had a hairdressing appointment so I had coffee alone with Bonny, he's a very easy person to be with and very entertaining. We were joined at lunchtime by Betty and Commander Patrick and we all lunched together at the officer's club. In the afternoon, Bet and I went shopping and seemed to spend a lot of money on nothing in particular, I bought a cigarette holder and stupidly didn't bother to see if a cigarette would fit in it – it didn't but I managed to stick adhesive tape on the holder! I had the usual Saturday feeling and managed to get through the show somehow. We had promised to go to the club to say farewell to the Navy. It was absolutely impossible to dance and as the new orders were in operation, we had to leave at midnight. Bonny told me whilst dancing that he'd be going back into his 'shell' again next week and that I had performed the miracle of bringing him out of it – a charming compliment! I do hope though, that he doesn't come over to Bruges. Allan,

Marj and Edna were out at a party and we had the key. At about 1.30 am, Betsy and I tip-toed to the front door, locked it and put the key through the dining room window onto the ledge. And so to bed. Goodnight. The shirt's a great success.

February 18th Sunday 1945

Kay knocked us up at 7.30 am, it was still quite dark. My first thought was about the key, so I popped into the girls' room and I was relieved to see Edna there. Our pick up was 9.30 am and to our great amazement, we left punctually and arrived at the Hotel Osborn – our hostel at 10.30 am. It is a very beautiful hotel with an excellent chef and if it weren't for the presence of the Phil Green's noisy band boys, we might look forward to an unusually comfortable week. After an excellent lunch, we (all the girls and Allan) went to a football match. The army boys versus Bruges, we had a good seat and thoroughly enjoyed it. Of course, the army won 4 -0, but it was an excellent game. Hapgood was playing left-back and captained the team. We walked from the game through the town and I love it already! The chimes of the bell are enchanting and play at all times of the day. After supper (which was cold but excellent), we all sat in the lounge reading and listening to Peter Gray, the blind pianist. He has a beautiful voice besides being a most gifted pianist, and it was simply heavenly to sit back in an armchair. With soft lighting in the room and listening to the lovely music, it made me feel rather homesick. At 11.00 pm, I retired to my lovely soft bed, where I'm writing now. Goodnight and sweet dreams.

February 19th Monday 1945

This morning, I awoke to early morning tea – it was undrinkable, but the idea was alright. We made a tour of inspection of the town and eventually found a very charming coffee shop where we also had some choice cakes. After lunch, I fell asleep over my book and aroused myself sufficiently to have early tea. We left for Knokke at 5.00 pm and had a very interesting journey in a converted Jerry transport coach, no comfort and plenty of petrol fumes. We passed over three canals and by block houses and trenches, gun emplacements and watch towers blown to bits when the Germans evacuated. We saw the famous 'Mole'[27] and in the canal, a sunken ship. Many of the deserted houses were marked with numbers, which we learned were to give warning of mines. Arriving at Knokke[28] via Zeebrugge we found the casino, a colossal barn of a place – very modern and with signs of pre-war splendour. The stage was built for concerts, not shows and there were no second tabs. The audience was dreadful – the majority Canadians and I think it was the worst we've ever had. Afterwards, we went to the officer's mess for about half an hour. The mess

---

[27] The Ostend Mole was a well-known landmark, a long pier or breakwater extending into the sea, built to protect Ostend's harbour. It played an important role in naval and military operations during both World Wars. The Mole was heavily damaged and rebuilt multiple times, notably during World War I when the British attacked it in 1918 to block German U-boat access.

[28] After the city's liberation by Canadian forces in October 1944, Knokke was a key base for anti-aircraft defences, with British forces stationed there to protect against enemy air attacks. Several RAF squadrons, including Spitfire units, operated from the airfield, supporting missions across the region.

is in an exceptionally beautiful house, built and decorated by a Dutchman I should say, no glaring lights but, besides table and reading lamps, a central lantern with three large electric candles. An open fireplace surrounded by blue and white Dutch tiles and a spit with implements for roasting an ox. Beautiful furniture made for comfort too, and carpets worth a fortune! A billet with a bathroom to every bedroom and hot water too -paradise in fact. Goodnight darling, my face has been burning tonight.

February 20th Tuesday 1945

Arose after a perfect night's sleep, to find it raining. So, we had coffee at the same little shop and on the way back, Bet bought a few more bits and pieces. We set off at 1.00 pm to the military hospital at Donke, which before the war was the Sanitorium Elisabeth. We gave two shows at 2.30 pm and 5.30 pm and they were very good indeed – in between we were served with a very good tea which I didn't eat however, otherwise, I shouldn't have been able to work. As we left the hospital all the lights were shining from all the hundreds of windows and it made a wonderful sight. Returning to Bruges at 8.30 pm, we managed to see the last half of Phil Green's show and it was very good indeed. Peter's act, 'Songs at the Piano' was really terrific, and the audience insisted upon encore after encore. He has a beautiful, clean mic voice with that nostalgic quality that only very few singers possess. And so to bed, goodnight.

February 21st Wednesday 1945

Awoke to a beautiful sunshiny day and at 11.00 am we were taken by the proprietress of a little lace shop, to the factory where the beautiful and famous Fairy lace is made. It is a convent school where the children are taught from an early age by the nuns. When they reach the age of 14, making lace becomes their work (if they so desire) and we saw a room full of girls from about the age of about 14 to 20 singing with fresh clean voices, while their fingers, with lightning movement, worked the bobbins to the patterns they were producing. I have never seen such exquisite work and for our special benefit, they sang Auld Lang Syne and Polly Wolly Doodle in English. Our guide told me that they work from 7.00 am until dusk and earn approximately 5 francs an hour, which seems to me a scandalous wage, considering the colossal profits made by the shops! On the way back from the factory, we walked through the old part of the town over the canal and I am enchanted by the place.

This afternoon, I wrote a short note home and we again went out and bought some little lace butterflies and had ice cream at our favourite café. We travelled to Blankenberge[29] by army open truck and gave a good show to the RAF. We were entertained afterwards by the sergeants. Air Vice Marshall Steele was in the audience tonight and actually laughed! Alec

---

[29] After its liberation by Canadian troops in September 1944, Blankenberge, Belgium was used as a rest and recuperation area for the Allied forces. This is likely why ENSA performers were sent to this area. Its port facilities and railway connections which were still functioning at this time, also made it useful as a staging point, providing logistical support to transport supplies and personnel before the final advance into German occupied territory.

Furnell is over for the night and we were pleased to renew our acquaintance with him after our snow fight at Hasselt. I am very tired – so to bed. I hope I hear from J tomorrow. Goodnight.

February 22nd Thursday 1945

I have had a very quiet day as I have been feeling extra-ordinarily weary. I can't imagine why. We opened at the G.T. Bruges[30] tonight and had a marvellous audience. This is another first-class theatre and again, Morris enjoyed himself with the sets! After the show, when Phil Green's boys returned, we were again entertained by Dave (one of us!)

At about 12.30 am the mail arrived, and we received a batch of news from mummy, full of 'matches and despatches'[31] enclosing a letter from Lilly and also merely mentioning an interview with Peggy Shappero. I'm curious to know what that was all about! I also at last, heard from Ruth and she enclosed a cutting

---

[30] The Grand Théâtre in Bruges, Belgium, served as a venue where ENSA (Entertainments National Service Association) performers entertained Allied troops and officers. This theatre, known locally as the Grote Schouwburg, was a prominent cultural centre in Bruges. During World War II, especially after the liberation of Belgium in late 1944, venues like this were often repurposed to boost the morale of military personnel through live performances.

[31] "Matches and Dispatches" is a traditional British phrase referring to the weddings, engagements, and death announcements in newspapers. "Matches" represents marriages and engagements, while "Dispatches" refers to deaths and obituaries. The phrase is sometimes expanded to "Hatches, Matches, and Dispatches", including births as well. It was a common way to describe the family announcements section, where people shared major life events.

about Freda's gallant 'adventure' at Walcheren. Sylvia wrote thanking us for the perfume and I was relieved to know that it had arrived safely. I am really longing to have an all-night gossip with mummy – I think it will take us a week to say all we want. I was disappointed not hearing from Jack but I know I'll hear from him soon. And so to bed. Goodnight.

I forgot to mention that Bill from Eindhoven came over to see Edna and surprised us all by seeing the show right through. The padre is on leave in England.

February 23rd Friday 1945

I stayed in all morning and answered the letters I received last night. My last post home – I hope! After lunch, Joe returned just as Bet and I were going out. We bought two, very pretty table centres and a handkerchief each, then we met Peter and Miff and helped them to buy presents. I made an appointment with a chiropodist for tomorrow.

I'm still feeling extremely weary and have come to the conclusion that it must be the air here that is so enervating.

Another excellent audience, after which, supper and early to bed. Bet stayed up talking with the boys, and I finished reading 'An Eye for a Tooth' in bed – an excellent modern tale by Dornford Yates. Goodnight.

February 24th Saturday 1945

Bet had the morning out with Dave and I intended to stay in and pack however, the sun was too much for me and I dressed and went for a walk, eventually meeting the gang for coffee in the usual shop. This morning the bells were playing the Wedding March and another well-known song – I can't remember the name.

I had an appointment with a chiropodist at 2.30 pm and I found him a charming little man with wonderful hands and he put me out of my misery in no time, and he only charged me 30 francs for the operation. I was most impressed.

I had just started packing about an hour before tea when we were paid a visit by Auntie Gertie's nephew, Gerald Ash. He is a most handsome young man and we had a pleasant chat. He saw the show at the hospital we played at Donke. He is stationed there in the R.A.M.C.[32] He left at tea time and I was sorry we couldn't invite him to the meal, but rules cannot be broken in this hostel so we said goodbye to him.

After quite a good show we packed up and, supper over, sat talking to the boys until 2.30 am. And so to bed, hardly able to keep my eyes open. Goodnight.

---

[32] R.A.M.C. Royal Army Medical Corps in the British army are responsible for providing medical care to soldiers in war and peacetime. During World War II, R.A.M.C. personnel worked on the front lines, in field hospitals, and in military medical units, treating wounded soldiers and providing medical support. R.A.M.C. members were non-fighting.

February 25th Sunday 1945

We left Bruges in an open truck one hour late at 10.30 am and stopped at Ghent for a cup of tea and a stitch, then on again, eventually arriving at Scheers, Brussels at 2.15 pm. After an excellent lunch, I kept myself awake looking out of the window at the passers by until the mail arrived. We were both surprised to find our photos in the local rag, as well as a long write up – local fame at last! Jack wrote me a long letter and made me happy again – bless him.

This evening we went with Betsy to the ENSA cinema to see Eleanor Powel in 'Sensations of 1945' and it was very weak. I am writing this in bed after a beautiful hot bath, and I'm feeling human again. We have a nice bedroom with bathroom adjoining and when the heat is on we shall enjoy ourselves. Goodnight.

February 26th Monday 1945

We arose at 9.30 am and made our toilet in the dark as the electricity only comes on at 5.30 pm with the heating system. After breakfast, we went to the theatre and found our dressing rooms on the 6th floor and unpacked. Another beautiful theatre with lifting orchestra pit and a revolving stage. An excellent surface for the dancing for which we are truly grateful.

Lunch over we went shopping and shop gazing with Betsy and Edna, each of us bought a pair of wooden soled summer shoes. Exhausted after our purchasing, we called into a convenient café and refreshed ourselves with ice cream – delicious!

Allan has strained his stomach and could not work, consequently, the timing went to hell, wished Marjorie in Timbuctoo for her neglect and stupidity … MD[33] my foot!! We had a very thin audience because all British troops had been confined to barracks in order to catch all absentees and after the show, army officers checked all soldiers leaving the theatre. All in all, it was a hateful evening and I sincerely hope that Allan is well enough to work tomorrow.

Brussels is another London complete with yanks. The shops and buildings are wonderful but I shall be glad to see the end of this week nevertheless! I have been feeling thoroughly bad tempered and depressed this evening so I'll close the book now. Goodnight. I forgot to mention we had more photos taken this afternoon.

February 27th Tuesday 1945

I have so much to write about today that I must start now before I forget all the places and things I have done. There were more warnings this morning - but I was asleep! At 8.15 am we were awakened with morning tea and electric lights, we enjoyed both and rejoiced to think that the light would be working today. At 10.00 am precisely, Maurice (who used to be manager at the Trocadero, London[34]), took Bet, me, Mona, Morris, Jack and Max Carroll on a tour of Brussels. We started at the Wiertz

---

[33] A Musical Director (MD) ensures the music runs smoothly, keeping the performers, musicians, and crew in sync. Sometimes, they may also be the conductor and set the tempo of the music.

[34] The Trocadero in Piccadilly Circus, was one of London's most elegant social venues. It had a luxurious restaurant and ballroom and provided live entertainment. It originally opened in 1896.

Museum and were fortunate in seeing about six of the colossal paintings of Antoine Wiertz. On entering the gallery, I was stricken with awe at the size, colours and magnificence of the canvases. The subjects are so complete in every detail that I was standing speechless, just staring. The museum is the house where Wiertz lived and worked and besides being a great artist with paint, he was a great musician – a genius!

On leaving there, Maurice conducted us to the monument of La Brabacrous and then to the tomb of the unknown warrior, from that point we could see all the roofs of Brussels. Next, we made our way through side streets, all the while shop gazing, to the market place on one side of which is the kings house and on the other side the town hall. The architecture in beautiful and this market place is supposed to be one of the best in the world. We went inside the cathedral and I was most impressed by the statue of Lady of Lourdes of which I have read, but on the whole this cathedral to my mind, cannot compare with that of Ripon or Winchester or York. Then we saw Manikin. We finished up, gratefully drinking a beer at a large café opposite La Bourse and then Bet and I went on our own to see the Theatre De La Monnaie where the Saddlers Wells ballet have played.

The shops here are full of the most exquisite things and since the people are all well dressed and seem to be short of nothing, I can't help thinking that they had few scruples about collaborating! We returned to Scheers for lunch completely exhausted. We had no sooner finished lunch that Bet dragged me out again to walk the food down, as she put it!

The show went very well tonight with a full house and Allan back! The six flights of stairs are getting me down – I'm utterly weary and two shows tomorrow. Max Carroll is too funny for words and it's good to have someone to laugh with and at.

Goodnight.

February 28th Wednesday 1945

At 10.15 am Allan phoned and asked me to go for a walk with him – I was still in bed reading. At just after 10.30 am we went out walking! We were tempted and had a cherry sundae each and then found our way to Rue De La Caserne by tram and foot to the Jewish Services Club. On our way back from there we met Charles the pianist from Ostend and he insisted on taking us to a very nice bar for an aperitif. We returned to Scheers where Edna was waiting for Charles and we all went out to Benny's for another aperitif. We apologised to Maurice for being late for lunch and found Scotch Tom, Capt. Foster and Megan waiting for us. Bet took Megan to the theatre whilst I swallowed some food and said hello to the other visitors.

We had a handful of people to the matinee and the show cut to bits! Megan is going into hospital tomorrow for an operation. At tea time, Bill arrived from Eindhoven for 48 hours, and complicated things considerably for Edna. He saw the show again – what courage! After the show, Bill left us and Edna, Allan, Betsy and I went with Charles to a little cosy bar (by the back entrance), where we drank advocaat and had two fried eggs each, plus plenty of dope from Charles about his fortnight in jail and his activities with the Marquis. We left at 1.00 am with our hands full of real eggs. And so to bed. Goodnight.

4

March 1945

March 1st Thursday 1945

I stayed in this morning whilst Bet went to meet Leonard. I bathed and washed my hair. After lunch, I went to the theatre to watch a rehearsal of The Belgian Boy, under the direction of Sidney Lipton. It is an excellent show, composed mainly of a first class Tzigane Orchestra and a very young soprano with an exquisite voice and a very good dancing act.

The show this evening was very good, although the tabs closed on us after our first number – never a dull moment!

I was very busy at the theatre tonight, ironing my smalls. Marjorie told me that she has to go into hospital for some internal operation, so it seems we might still be going home at the weekend. Of course, the great J is doing his damnedest to make events go his way! Goodnight.

March 2nd Friday 1945

I went to see the dress rehearsal of the Belgian show this morning and after lunch, we played a matinee to a handful of people. Just a waste of time and energy. Between shows, I went with Allan to partake of ice cream and made myself thoroughly cold. The evening show was very good I retired quite soon after supper and had a hot bath – what comfort! Quite an ordinary day. Goodnight.

March 3rd Saturday 1945

At 10.00 am sharp, Betty, Allan, Maurice and I set out into the rain for more sightseeing. First, we went to the Senate House and I was struck by the simple grandeur of the white marble stone. We were shown in the House of Commons and then the House of Lords, in the latter the ceiling is covered with the coat of arms of each county in gold, a most impressive and beautiful sight. We were each given as souvenirs, a sheet of paper and envelope with the Senate crest. In the royal room are the most beautiful busts of the royal family in marble. From there we visited the Palace of Justice which was partially destroyed by fire when the Germans tried to burn incriminating evidence. It is now being repaired. On the way through the park, we passed the Royal Palace, another impressive building but from the outside I prefer Buckingham Palace. We had no sooner finished lunch than Stan Willis-Croft walked in and of course, we fell on his neck! We went with him to meet his gang and had a most hilarious afternoon until they departed to work.

Returning for tea, we had another surprise, Victor and George had come over from Eindhoven. Victor was so glad to see us, he had just returned from leave in the UK and he was hoping to take us all back to Eindhoven tomorrow, but he was disappointed to learn that we had already arranged to meet Stan. Some mail arrived today from Jack and Kay and Freda, telling me that Bab's new baby had died – How very sad after so long. Auntie Flo's doing her best for me bless her[35].

The show went very well tonight and we packed up a parcel for Max Carroll to take to the family for us in Paris[36] and I am making a few enquiries about our chances of getting there. Goodnight.

March 4th Sunday 1945

Stan came around at about 10.30 am and we went with him to the Cap du Nord for a drink and a gossip. Hordes of people have arrived at Scheers[37] today and we have been relegated to the lounge for lunch. After lunch, Bet and I went for a walk in the rain, spent an hour in the ENSA news theatre and finished

---

[35] This comment is likely referring to Rita's Aunt trying to smooth over the family's views about Rita having a non-Jewish boyfriend, which was met with disapproval.

[36] *Rita's father's brother settled in Paris after their emigration from Poland, Rita's parents settled in England.*

[37] Grand Hôtel G. Scheers was an Art Deco hotel in Brussels, located on Boulevard Adolphe Max 132. Designed by Edmond Libion, it was built in 1930 and featured arched windows, elegant balconies, and a stylish restaurant on the first floor.

During its prime, it was a popular place to stay, used to host military personnel and entertainers during World War II. The hotel was an unusual and distinctive L-shape, with a natural stone façade and arched windows.

up eating ice cream in our own particular café. Stan and Peter Knight called for us at 7.00 pm and we went to see 'Impatient Years' with Jean Arthur and Lee Bowman – very good. Then we had supper with the boys at the Concordian and walked back to Scheers just before 12.00 pm. It's been grand seeing Stan, almost like old times - with more laughs. And so to bed after a quick bath. Goodnight.

March 5th Monday 1945

A good beginning of the day, a little letter from Jack in reply to mine that Betsy's Jamie took to England. Stan came around at about 11.30 am to say goodbye and we promised to call in on his people when we get home.

After lunch we went out shopping with Betsy and bought some theatrical powder (10% discount). We went again and I bought an unusual white mask brush that I christened 'Ferrier', because of its resemblance to Betsy when she puts on her 'dead pan' makeup. I also purchased a dainty pair of white shoes for Freda's baby and I hope they fit her. We collected Allan, and we went to the usual shop for ice cream. We had a busman's holiday this evening and went to see 'Showpiece', this week's show, at the Variety Theatre. Just before the curtain rang up, Jack had an epileptic fit and Allan had to take him to hospital. Is it possible for anything else to happen to us before we get home? Jim has been advised to stop working for a month at least, and by the looks of things now, a good holiday wouldn't do any of us any harm! The show was, on the whole, very good, completely carried by Devine & King. The girl's dresses were really lovely and again, I cannot understand why our show was denied new costumes, 'Happy Hikers', from the viewpoint of all-round entertainment, is a far better show.

I hope we hear something definite very soon, this unaccustomed inactivity doesn't suit me over here – inactivity at home however is another matter entirely. Goodnight.

March 6th Tuesday 1945

It has been raining most of the day and I stayed in bed most of the morning as I was feeling rather low and I hadn't anything to do anyway!

After lunch we went to the cinema to see 'Since You Went Away' with Claudette Colbert, Monty Woolley, Jennifer Jones and Shirley Temple etc. It was very good indeed but very sad and I cried gallons. At the end of the film, most of the men were blowing their noses too!

This evening we all went to the Garrison Theatre and saw 'Love in a Mist' A good company, a good play and a thoroughly enjoyable evening. I learned tonight that Colin is taking Freda and Marion home tomorrow, I don't think it's fair! I'm absolutely full of impatience to get home and I'm longing to see Jack. Goodnight.

March 7th Wednesday 1945

This morning, Bet and I had a good prowl around, and after, we had a delicious and most expensive coffee. It was necessary as the morning tea was conspicuous by its absence this morning. We bought mummy a pair of stockings – nice ones but we were stung for 'em! Marion and Freda departed this morning and left a volcano erupting in the office.

After lunch, I wrote a long letter to Jack and then the two 'Betties' and I went to the Montgomery Club for tea. It is the Palais D'Egemont, a very beautiful building in the Place Royale, taken over by the NAAFI. A good small orchestra played in the restaurant and there is also a special 'Ladies Wing' with every comfort, plus a hairdresser!

From there, we went to the Palais des Beaux-Arts and heard the Belgian National Orchestra conducted by Franz Andrie. They played a delightful programme, Bach, German's Nell Gwyn Dances, Tchaikovsky's Nutcracker Suite, Pavane by Ravel and Beethoven's 5th Symphony. I loved it all, and the way they played 'The King' was an education. Fortunately, Felix had the 'tilly', so we got a lift back to Scheers. I've really enjoyed today and all being well we might be moving on Friday. Goodnight darling.

March 8th Thursday 1945

This morning we had elevenses, hot chocolate and fresh buns with Felix at the Officer's teashop and very nice it was too.

This afternoon, Bet and I took ourselves to the Theatre Du

Monde to see and hear the opera 'Sapho'. We were surprised to have such good stall seats for 28 francs each and we enjoyed the show thoroughly. The music by Massenet was beautifully played by a most competent orchestra and both the singing and the acting of the artists was excellent. I understood it completely, despite the fact that the opera was in French. This opera house is very similar to those in Bruges and Ghent, everything is very formal and proper, and the ancient ushers are in white tie and tails and, as is the custom over here, no smoking allowed.

This is the very last day of our tour and on the whole, I have really enjoyed it. It has passed so quickly, and yet it seems so long ago since we left London. Why am I feeling depressed I wonder? There have been air-raid alarms all day long, but as usual, nobody takes any notice. According to the news, we have taken Cologne and everything is going very well. I wonder if we will do the Orkney's tour? I have packed and am feeling very tired. Goodnight.

March 9th Friday 1945

We were ready waiting for the transport at 9.30 am when word came through from H.Q. that we would not leave before 11.00 am.

At 1.00 pm, we had lunch and at 2.00 pm, the transport arrived and at 3.00 pm we set off. Five and a half hours of hanging around, disgusted and impatient.

We stopped at Ghent for a cup of tea frozen stiff and arrived at the Marion Hotel, Ostend at 7.30 pm. At 8.30 pm, we had dinner and then took ourselves off to the club to see Charles.

We were surprised to see Bonny and Tony, who had had a phone message from Phil Burton, telling them of our arrival. It was quite like old times and they were delighted to see us. Capt. Hopper was also there and gave me messages for Phil Lavine. We returned to the Marion to find George Ebrick and Co. in possession of the lounge.

And so to bed.

March 10th Saturday 1945

We had very little sleep last night, waiting to be called at 7.00 am. The truck eventually got us down to the dock at 9.00 am after knocking down a couple of wheel barrows on the way and getting onto the wrong dock first. Bonny came to say goodbye before going on duty. Again, there was an hour's delay while it was decided whether there would be room for us on the boat. 200 Dutch children were being taken to England to homes in Hull and Coventry and they embarked first. We eventually embarked and set sail at 10.00 am. A beautiful sunny day, cold of course but a very good crossing. A corvette passed us and made a fine sight ploughing through the water in the sunshine. We had a hilarious meal at lunchtime of bread and marg' and a hunk of spam, plus a handful of sweets.

We docked at 7.00 pm, and we were all greatly relieved when, instead of having all our baggage searched as expected, the customs officer merely asked us what we had and let it go at that! We left Tilbury and arrived at the ENSA hostel, London at 9.45 pm, tired, hungry and rather forlorn. I immediately rang home and surprised mummy. Why is homecoming never as exciting as one always imagines it to be? If only Jack could have been waiting for me - I should have been happy; I am so worried! And so, to NAAFI bed.

March 11th Sunday 1945

Betsy, Betty and I, have had the day out. We breakfasted at the Old Vienna café and kept calling the waitress 'mademoiselle'. We called at the ENSA garage, collected our luggage and dumped it at Kings Cross to save time tomorrow. After lunch, I phoned Jack. It was lovely to speak to him, but we were cut off again, and I was disappointed. At 3.30 pm, we met Auntie Annie and Uncle and went out to tea with them. They were delighted to see us and we had to tell them about the tour, I can see we're going to get sick of repeating everything very soon. The three of us then went to see Dianne Durban in 'Can't Help Singing' and enjoyed it thoroughly. And that's that, please God, let us get home tomorrow. Goodnight.

March 12th Monday 1945

We arrived at 'The Lane'[38] as arranged at 11.00 am only to find that Mr Collins (couldn't or wouldn't) see us until 2.30 pm, which meant, of course, missing the only through train home. My feelings are unprintable! We had a sketchy lunch with Edna at Fulla's, I wired Jack and then at 2.30 pm Mr Collins told us in no uncertain terms that he had no further need of our services, so the conquering heroines return with the order of the boot! And that ends our successful BLA (British Liberation Army) tour. It is really quite a relief to be finished at last with J.L. and partner and I have a feeling he is responsible for the breaking up of the show. Edna promised to see to our props and we caught the 5.30 pm train and arrived home well after midnight. Mummy and Dad are both well, although mummy has been worrying constantly about me and Jack. We had more tears before we eventually retired about 3.30 am.

March 13th Tuesday 1945

I awoke at 9.00 am with a bad head and I have been feeling weary and worried all day. Jack phoned me this morning. It left me utterly wretched. What is to become of this mess? I hate myself for hurting mummy and dad, and yet how can I help

---

[38] We believe 'The Lane' references the Theatre Royal, Drury Lane. One of London's most famous and historic theatres. It is located on Drury Lane in the Covent Garden area and has been a significant part of London's theatrical scene since the 17th century. During World War II, the Theatre Royal Drury Lane served as the headquarters for the Entertainments National Service Association (ENSA) and was under the management of ENSA, with W. J. MacQueen-Pope overseeing publicity operations.

loving him so much? They won't understand. This afternoon, we entertained a flow of visitors: Mrs Tate, Freda and the baby and Mrs Brown with daughter-in-law. Mrs Schwartz and a very 'adult' Audrey came to tea, and now a solo school is in progress with Maurice and Jack. I do not think I shall continue this diary further and it seems another chapter is ended.

Hull Girls with E.N.S.A.—Two young Hull girls had a lucky escape recently when the E.N.S.A. party to which they are attached hit a German mine over on the Western Front. They are Rita and Betty Ernstein, known as "The Erwin Sisters," who are now with the big outfit called "The Happy Hikers." The story of how one of the young dancers tragically lost her life in this accident has already been told

RITA AND BETTY

nationally, but "the show must go on," and so with half their number in hospital the company carried on with their work of entertaining the troops.

Rita and Betty, daughters of Mr and Mrs H. Ernstein, of 61, Glencoe-st., Hull, are two smart dancers with very twinkling toes who have been tapping since they were tiny-tots.

It has always been their ambition to go on the stage, and although they had done a certain amount of professional work, they had contented themselves principally with local cabarets, concerts, until the war came and with it their great chance. For the first three years they spent all their spare time entertaining the troops with one of the popular voluntary shows operating under V.E.S. Northern Command, and just over two years ago volunteered and were accepted by E.N.S.A.

In Belgium Now.—Since that time they have toured England, Scotland and Wales, giving shows for the troops and factory workers, and just before Christmas went abroad with "The Happy Hikers," a party of 18 artists. They haven't had an easy time either in England or abroad, for sometimes accommodation has been mediocre to say the least of it, and since they have been "over there" they have had to rough it more than once. At the present time they are working with an 11-piece band in a huge opera house somewhere in Belgium. They tell their mother that this is the acme of comfort, that the stage is so big you could lose a grand piano in a corner of it, and in the auditorium is one of those magnificent crystal chandeliers reminiscent of "The Phantom of the Opera." They even have a wardrobe mistress at the moment to wash and iron for them!

Hull Daily Mail Newspaper clipping

MARCH 1945

5

April 1945

April 2nd Easter Monday 1945

The past three weeks have been filled with happiness and utter misery for me, but at last, I really believe that Jack and I will be together for good, very soon. I had a wonderful week with him when he was on leave, the more I am with him and know of him, the more I love him. I am sure we should be very happy together. Please God all will be well!

Harold has returned to finish his service in India, and we are again in London rehearsing more new people into the show, now entitled 'High Heels and Hicks'.[39] Edna and Kay are not with us now. We are going out on the Orkney tour, but I have no heart for it, and I'm praying peace will be declared before we set out. It is expected anytime time now, and everyone this Easter has felt more than just the holiday spirit. I can't imagine

---

[39] Still part of ENSA, Rita and her sister Betty are preparing for another tour as part of a company with a new show called 'High Heels and Hicks'

peacetime except when I think of Jack, I do hope he's not feeling too miserable after having all his teeth out – and they looked so good, too!

April 10th Tuesday 1945

Well, this is the second day of the Scotland tour. I spent the weekend in Hull and Jack came with Auntie Flo. He was complete with new teeth and bless him, he was coping bravely, they look very good thank goodness. Mummy was insistent upon us waiting six months until the end of the tour, but we have decided that if the war ends soon we will get married then. I don't want to wait, I so wanted us to start life together in the summer time. I arrived for the show at 8.00 pm last night at Bellsdyke hospital, Larbert, after travelling back from Glasgow from 7.00 o'clock in the morning, and I was completely worn out.

Today we travelled to this worker's hostel (memories of munitions), where we stayed until Saturday, although we only work in the theatre here tonight. Benny Cotton[40] is with us again driving the coach and I was glad to see him again, still mobbed by the women!

---

[40] Benny Cotton was a bassist and vocalist. After the war, he made a name with the group The Dozier Boys. He also worked with Andrew Tibbs and pianist Sonny Blount (later known as Sun Ra). He shared lead vocals on tracks such as "In a Traveling Mood." The group released singles like "She Only Fools with Me" and "St. Louis Blues" under the Aristocrat label in 1949.

April 11th Wednesday 1945

Show to RAF at Turnberry[41] and on the way we passed over the electric brae[42] via Prestwick and Ayre.

The opening of the show is still rather feeble but the boys enjoyed the show on the whole. Afterwards, we had supper and were entertained in the officer's mess. Returned to the hostel about 2.00 am.

---

[41] In April 1945, RAF Turnberry was an important airfield near Turnberry, South Ayrshire, Scotland, primarily used for training pilots in Coastal Command and RAF Ferry Command. Originally built during World War I, it was repurposed for World War II, where it played a key role in preparing pilots to operate aircraft like the Bristol Beaufighter and the Vickers Wellington, commonly used for maritime patrols and anti-submarine warfare. The airfield also supported aircraft movements across the Atlantic as part of RAF Ferry Command. As the war neared its end, RAF Turnberry's training operations began to wind down, marking a transition toward peacetime activities.

[42] During World War II, the Electric Brae in South Ayrshire, Scotland, became a popular attraction among military personnel stationed nearby. Located on the A719 coastal road near Ayr and Prestwick, it creates the optical illusion that vehicles roll uphill when left in neutral, even though they are actually moving downhill, due to the surrounding landscape. The phenomenon occurs because the horizon and land slopes create a misleading perspective, making the downhill slope appear as if it is an incline.

It is reported that General Dwight D. Eisenhower, who had a residence at Culzean Castle, would often take guests to witness this intriguing phenomenon. American servicemen from the Prestwick airbase frequently visited the site, captivated by the illusion of vehicles seemingly defying gravity.

April 12th Thursday 1945

Worked to the Gordon Highlanders on the race course at Ayre. We were not expected and the accommodation was nil but they were a very good audience. We were well entertained by the officers afterwards – President Roosevelt died today.

April 13th Friday 1945

A lovely day – received a letter from Jack and replied immediately whilst doing the first spot of sunbathing. Show at HMS Scotia[43] – expected a party like last time, but most disappointed. Bath at 2.00 am

April 14th Saturday 1945

Returned to Glasgow – Show at Shanda – not bad – stuffy mess afterwards.

---

[43] HMS Scotia was a Royal Navy shore-based training site in Ayr, Scotland, from 1942 to 1948. It was established on a former Butlins holiday camp, mainly training naval personnel in communications. After the war, it was returned to Butlins in 1946 and later became the Craig Tara Caravan Park.

Entertainment was an important part of life at HMS Scotia, with ENSA organising performances to entertain the trainees and to boost the morale of the staff there. One account from 1942 mentions an ENSA production of 'Hay Fever' featuring Ellen Pollock, although apparently, high demand for tickets made attending a challenge. A memorial now stands at the site to honour its wartime role.

April 15th Sunday 1945

Left for Greenock immediately after lunch and played a good matinee at the King's Theatre[44], then on to Sulcoates for the evening show at the Regal cinema. A beautiful drive along the Clyde side through Gourock and Largs. The destroyers, aircraft carriers and cruisers on the Clyde made a wonderful sight in the sunshine, with the Isle of Annan in the distance. Horace Collins[45] (God!) came to see Jim and Marion in the show, so we did a full show for a change! Goodnight darling.

---

[44] The King's Theatre in Greenock, originally opened as the Alexandra Theatre in 1905, was a prominent venue in the town's cultural scene. Around 1910, it was renamed the King's Theatre. The theatre hosted various productions, including the play "Isabel, Edward and Anne" by Barry O'Brien from 9th to 14th November 1925. Over the years, the building underwent several transformations, eventually becoming the Odeon Cinema.

[45] Horace Collins was a prominent figure in Scottish variety theatre and played a significant role during World War II as the Scottish Regional Controller and Chairman of the Entertainments National Service Association (ENSA). In this capacity, he was responsible for organising entertainment to boost the morale of armed forces, the Merchant Navy, munitions workers, dock workers, and hospital staff across Scotland. His efforts included dispatching performance groups overseas to entertain Scottish troops abroad. For his tireless charitable work and contributions during the war, Horace Collins was awarded an OBE in 1946.

In January 1940, Collins arranged for a travelling cinema show to visit a unit on the north side of Glasgow, further exemplifying his dedication to providing entertainment during challenging times.

His leadership and commitment significantly bolstered morale during the war years, making a lasting impact on Scottish entertainment and the broader community.

April 16th Monday 1945

Lovely day – disappointed no letter from Jack although lots from home. Show at hospital. Gartloch – small audience; short show, small stage. Missing you dreadfully tonight dearest, Goodnight and God bless.

April 17th Tuesday 1945

Early pick up for army show at Lanark -all young boys in training. Poor stage but excellent audience. No mess[46]!

April 18th Wednesday 1945

Up early and packed. Left for Inveraray at 2.30 pm, a very beautiful drive and a perfect day. We passed Loch Lomond and stopped for tea at Arrachar, a tiny village behind Loch Long. Went straight to the show at Inveraray and had a marvellous audience. Returned at last to the Stag Hotel, Lochgilphead.

---

[46] This references the Officer's Mess. A designated area within a military base, ship, or establishment where commissioned officers can socialise. The mess provides a space for meals, recreation, and official gatherings. All ENSA personnel were given officer status so that they could use the facilities of an officer's mess.

April 19th Thursday 1945

Lovely day after a good night's sleep in a real bed! Life at the Stag Head is very pre-war! Found an excellent coffee shop then after lunch went for a lovely walk beside the Dinan Canal with Jack, Sid and Betsy. We parked ourselves in a field and all fell asleep sunbathing. Worked HMS Quebec[47] at Inveraray – Good mess.

April 20th Friday 1945

Coffee again at the same little café. Left at 2.30 pm after buying ice-cream, and arrived at Machaihanish camp at 4.00 pm. Two shows, the second one full – mess afterwards. We stayed on the

---

[47] HMS Quebec near Inveraray, Scotland, was a Royal Navy training base, serving as the Combined Operations Training Centre (CTC). Established in 1940, it played a crucial role in preparing Navy, Army, and Air Force personnel for amphibious warfare, including the D-Day landings.

Throughout World War II, around 250,000 troops from Britain, the US, Canada, France, Poland, and Norway trained there in landing craft operations, beach assaults, and coordinated joint force operations. The base's strategic importance was underscored by notable visitors, including King George VI, Winston Churchill, and Lord Mountbatten.

HMS Quebec closed in June 1946. Today, the site is home to Argyll Caravan Park, with a memorial honouring those who trained there and the many who never returned.

camp in the Wren's[48] quarters and shared a 'cabin' with Joyce and Mavis.

April 21st Saturday 1945

Frozen stiff all night. Arose at 7.00 am and had a hot bath. Breakfasted with the Wren officers and then went into Campbeltown. Wrote to Jack over coffee and had lunch at the Royal Hotel. After lunch, we went to see James Mason in 'Hotel Reserve'. Two shows at HMS Nimrod[49] – very good, returned to the Wrennery.

---

[48] Women's Royal Naval Service (WRNS), commonly known as the Wrens, played a vital role in the British war effort. Initially established in 1917, the service was reformed in 1939, growing rapidly to support the Royal Navy. By the war's peak, over 75,000 Wrens were serving in a wide range of roles.

Although they were not sent to sea in combat, Wrens took on crucial jobs in communications, intelligence, coding and cyphers, radar operations, aircraft maintenance, transport, and administration. Some worked at Bletchley Park, assisting in codebreaking efforts, while others operated coastal and overseas bases, including HMS Quebec, where they trained in amphibious operations.

Their contributions helped free up men for frontline duties, and their efficiency and professionalism led to the WRNS becoming a permanent part of the Royal Navy in 1949.

[49] In 1945, HMS Nimrod was a Royal Navy shore base in Campbeltown, Argyll, Scotland. Established during World War II, it served as the principal anti-submarine training base, providing specialised instruction in anti-submarine warfare techniques. It enhanced the Royal Navy's capabilities against the German U-boat threat.

April 22nd Sunday 1945

Coach journey to Falkirk, stopped at The Stag, Lochgilphead for lunch and Glasgow for tea. Eventually arrived at this dreadful miner's hostel at 5.30 pm.

April 23rd Monday 1945

Lovely day – went with the girls and Sid and Jack to Edinburgh. Phoned my Jack and had a lovely chat. Toured the shops and bought amber earrings and went to see Irene Dunn and Charles Boyer in 'Together Again' Sid had his wallet pinched, returned to the hostel and early to bed.

April 24th Tuesday 1945

Bad news from home about Daddy, feeling utterly wretched. Show at Port Edgar to Navy – very good but stuffy mess afterwards.

The base adapted to evolving naval warfare tactics as the war progressed. Personnel trained at HMS Nimrod were instrumental in safeguarding Allied maritime operations during the latter stages of the conflict.

April 25th Wednesday 1945

Train journey to Cupa, Fife, a good hostel. Naval show somewhere near the Fourth Bridge - no mess! Two letters from Jack – more trouble.

April 26th Thursday 1945

Fine day -walked around Cupa and had some good coffee. Wrote letters. Naval show at Crail.

April 27th Friday 1945

Spent a lovely day at St Andrews with Bet, Jack and Betsy. RAF show at Leuchars – good. Invited to the officer's dance but it was so packed so we didn't stay – all the women in evening dress!!

April 28th Saturday 1945

Washed my hair (scalded myself into the bargain) and had a bath. Fine day – Navy show at Rosythe -no mess. Row with Jim about the baggage – I won!

April 29th Sunday 1945

Arrived for lunch at the Adelphi Hotel, Glasgow – snowing, miserable day and early to bed. Stinking cold.

April 30th Monday 1945

Bought my slacks at Rowans – coffee at Cadira and left at 12.30pm for Newton Stewart. RAF show at West Freugh, Stranrear. Sgts mess. Very tired – Letters from Jack and home.

6

May 1945

May 1st Tuesday 1945

Cold day – coffee at Stuarty Dairies – nice little village.

May 2nd, 3rd, 4th, 5th and 6th not recorded.

May 7th Sunday 1945

I travelled from Newton Stewart to Locherbrie via Dumfries to meet my Jack, as having missed his connection at Newcastle. I could see no way for him to reach Newton Stewart that day. However, he arrived at 6.00 pm, nearly an hour late, by which time he had missed both last busses to Dumfries and Newton Stewart. I did manage to secure a taxi, and we eventually and very comfortably, fixed up for the night at the Station Hotel, Dumfries. On seeing each other again, the troubles seemed to roll away and we were happy!

After an excellent dinner, we had a walk around the town and into the country. It was a fine evening, and we sat on a roadside seat and listened to the birds and the animal life around us. We were enveloped in peace, and it was good. Returning to the hotel at 10.30 pm we had a nightcap cup of tea in the lounge – alone again, enjoying our own company. If only it could always be so! And so to bed and the precious good night.

May 8th Monday 1945

At 2.00 am this morning, whilst I was sleeping, Germany signed an unconditional surrender to the Allies. When our company arrived at Glasgow today, flags and bunting decorated the streets and everything was set to celebrate VE (Victory in Europe) day, I immediately phoned Jack about joining the show and I hope with all my heart that Collins will agree. My face is healing and I'm feeling much more optimistic now. We travelled to a naval camp at Ayre to find the place deserted, so we were invited to the wardroom instead of giving a show and they made a party.

At 9.00 pm we learned that officially V.E. day is tomorrow and a complete holiday! I did not stay to the party but returned to the hostel by bus. On our way through Glasgow all the lights went up and the city square was a wonderful sight. All the trees were hung with fairy lights, and great arc lamps illuminated the university and other important buildings. The people have torn down the six-year old-black outs[50] and brightness is everywhere. Children have made huge bonfires in all the streets, but it is still difficult to realise that it is, at long last, over in Europe – the future suddenly feels frightening but if I'm with Jack, I shall have no fear!

Strange that on May 8th 1941 at 2.00 am we were blasted out of 567 Anlaby Road[51] I am waiting for the girls and Betty to come in, it is now 1.00 am. Edna Welsh left the show today.

May 9th Tuesday 1945 – VE Day

May 16th Wednesday 1945 – Jack's Birthday

We are in Kirkwall, Orkney, our third day here after a sick-making journey – I was just not sick! I am feeling very happy as Jack is coming to join the show any day now and I am getting very excited. We are all living in an army hut with our own

---

[50] There were blackout regulations enforced across Britain to prevent enemy bombers from spotting towns and cities at night. To block the light from shining out of houses and businesses, people used thick blackout curtains, heavy fabric or cardboard; some painted their windows. Streetlights were switched off, and car headlights were dimmed with slitted covers. Wardens patrolled to ensure no light escaped, as even a small glimmer could guide enemy aircraft.

[51] 567 Anlaby Road, Hull, was the former family home of the Ernstein family - Rita and her sister Betty with their parents Hirsch and Rachael. On the nights of 7th and 8th May 1941, Kingston upon Hull endured some of its most devastating air raids, resulting in nearly 400 fatalities and extensive destruction across the city.

dining room, lounge and bedrooms and it's rather comfy. I like Kirkwall, there is a good coffee shop here fortunately. The town is quite small but there's a harbour. All the shops are closed so we had coffee in the NAAFI today, I also received Jack's letter from last Tuesday.

The show went extremely well last night, so our Orkney tour is likely to be a success. The atmosphere in the company now is grand, so different from that on the BLA[52] tour.

May 28th Monday 1945

Jack has been with us now at Kirkwall for four days and everything is fine. He has just realised that Kay loves him – he is so lovable!

---

[52] BLA probably refers to the informal term 'British Liberation Army', given to the troops from the British forces involved in the final stages of the war in mainland Europe, namely France, Belgium, the Netherlands, and Germany after the Normandy landings.

A N.A.A.F.I. SHOW

'COME THE THREE CORNERS
OF THE WORLD IN ARMS,
AND WE SHALL SHOCK THEM.'

ORGANISED
BY

E. N. S. A.

7

June 1945

June 4th Monday 1945 – Jack bought the ring today

'Jack' Algiers, ENSA tour 1944

June 8th Friday 1945

This is the eve of my wedding day. It is hard to believe that at last Jack and I are going to be married, but I am very happy and please God, I hope that we shall always be happy together. We played the Dunluce Castle tonight and we went down to see the inside of the submarine Sea Devil. We shall be going there tomorrow night to a party and I shall be Mrs Stewart! Dear God let us always love each other and make me a good wife.

June 9th Saturday 1945 – Derby Day – My Wedding Day!

We crossed to Kirkwall by the 8.30 am drifter and the sun was shining on us. We were married by the registrar at 12.30 pm and Bet managed to get me a bouquet of beautiful sweet peas. We lunched with the company at the Ayre Hotel and were drenched with rain by a shower on the way there. We had wedding gifts of money from the whole company and all the staff have been very kind and helpful.

We celebrated in the evening by seeing the show from the front and I was thrilled, it was grand. Jimmy sent the girls down to the auditorium and dragged us both up onto the stage. Jack had to sing 'You Are My Hearts Delight' to me and bless him, he was great. It was a simply terrifying ordeal for us both!

Before retiring for the night, we discovered that our room had been turned upside down and our pyjamas and nightdress sewn up. Cornflakes and Allbran had been generously distributed in the beds and streamers hanging from the ceiling. A good time was had by all!

I am now and forever, Mrs Stewart.

MR. J. STEWART—MISS R. ERNSTEIN

The marriage took place at Kirkwall, Orkney, between John W. Stewart, of Chatham, and Rita Ernstein, of Hull (one of the Erwin Twins). They are members of an Ensa company, "High Heels and Hicks," and were granted a special licence by the High Sheriff of Orkney. All the company attended, including Major Whitmore, O.C. Entertainments, Orkney, and naval, military and civilian personnel from Chatham. The celebrations were held on board a battle cruiser and submarine.

Marriage newspaper clipping

June 21st Thursday 1945

We have just arrived in South Ronaldsay from Lyness[53] – a good trip by drifter although very windy. We are all glad indeed to have left Lyness hostel. Last night we had a lovely party on board the 'Caesei[54]' and the Commander and Captain entertained us the whole evening. This is our second week of married life and I am very happy. I have been busy writing the news to all the family and I am waiting for replies. Greetings wire from Ruth was waiting here.

July 1st Sunday 1945

During the past week I have received many charming letters from the family which have really completed my happiness.

On Wednesday we flew here, Lerwick, Shetland from Orkney

---

[53] Lyness (HMS Proserpine) on Hoy, was a key naval base during World War II, used by the Royal Navy's Home Fleet. Ships, including destroyers like HMS Caesar, frequently docked there for refuelling, maintenance, and resupply.

[54] In June 1945, **HMS Caesar**, a Ca-class destroyer, was actively engaged in naval operations. On June 6th, she participated in exercises off Plymouth with the submarine HMS Unrivalled. Later that day, HMS Caesar, alongside other destroyers, escorted HMS Jamaica, which had King George VI and Princess Elizabeth aboard, for an inspection of the Channel Islands.

By mid June, HMS Caesar was conducting anti-submarine exercises at Scapa Flow in the Orkney Islands with the submarine HMS Sea Devil. As she regularly used Lyness (HMS Proserpine), we believe this is vessel Rita was on board.

and we have played the GT[55] which is also the hostel where the girls are living. I like this place very much and our digs with Mrs Gairson are very good.

This morning Jack and I had a wonderful surprise, Mummy and daddy phoned and spoke to both of us, also Auntie Minnie chipped in, and we were very glad to notice that they all sounded much better.

Tonight, we travel to Sullum Voe for a show and tomorrow, to Sumburgh and on Wednesday we sail to Aberdeen and start work again in Edinburgh.

---

[55] The Garrison Theatre in Lerwick, Shetland, is a historic venue that could correspond to the initials "GT." Established in 1903/4 as the Lerwick Drill Hall and Gymnasium, it served as the headquarters for the 7th Volunteer Battalion Gordon Highlanders and functioned as a drill hall during World War I. In 1942, during World War II, the building was converted into a theatre by the Entertainments National Service Association (ENSA) to entertain troops stationed in Shetland, hosting notable performers such as George Formby and Gracie Fields.

ENSA badge

8

December 1945

December 17th Monday 1945

It is many months since I wrote the last chapter in this book. After completing the Scotland tour, we worked all Northern Ireland, peace was declared and we returned to England on October 13th.

We have been married six months now and Jack is the manager of the Woolwich Empire[56] and I am surprising myself daily by my accomplishments as a housewife. I must say that I enjoy keeping house and feel great satisfaction in the knowledge that Jack is so happy to return to me and our little home every evening and that every Sunday is a holiday.

He has had another severe attack of his stomach trouble and I have made him promise to have another X ray. It grieves me

---

[56] The Woolwich Empire was a well-known theatre and music hall in Woolwich, London, built in 1900 as part of the Moss Empires chain. It became a popular venue for variety performances, featuring comedians, singers, and dancers who entertained local audiences.

to see him suffering and to be able to do so little for him! I have just finished addressing Christmas cards and it seems as if a whole lifetime has passed in a flash since I started this diary almost a year ago.

At this time last year, I was in Darlington with Jack on embarkation leave before going to Holland. It all seems like a fantastic dream!

Really looking forward to my life with Jack. For the last time in this diary - goodnight!

Afterword

After training in Italy, Jack performed with The D'Oyly Carte Opera Company before spending over six years with the International Opera Company.

During World War II, he toured with an ENSA music and comedy show, entertaining troops in North Africa. While in Algeria, he even had the remarkable experience of acting as feed man to Humphrey Bogart. One of the greatest highlights of his career came in 1943, when he performed in front of Winston Churchill.

In 1944, Jack was part of the John Stewart ENSA Company, touring with Tommy Trinder in Malta. However, as the war came to an end, he faced a difficult decision—whether to continue his career as an opera singer or transition into a more stable life. The thought of long periods apart from Rita ultimately led him to embrace a new opportunity, using his wartime management skills in the theatre world.

John Stewart 'Jack' (far right) with Tommy Trinder, Malta 1944

After two successful years managing The Woolwich Empire in London, with Rita enjoying 'keeping house,' Jack was offered a new role in 1947. He became general manager of The Regent

Theatre in Rotherham, South Yorkshire—a small provincial theatre, just 60 miles from Rita's family in Hull. It was the perfect location and, in terms of entertainment, a blank canvas waiting to be transformed.

At The Regent, Jack brought spectacular productions to Rotherham audiences. He staged star-studded pantomimes, as well as full-scale circus performances featuring live animals—including bears and elephants! Variety shows became a guaranteed crowd-puller, featuring some of the biggest names of the time, including Frankie Vaughan, Max Bygraves, Jimmy Young, Winifred Atwell, and Bill Maynard.

Unfortunately, as television and cinema grew in popularity in the 1950s, many variety theatres across Britain struggled and the Regent Theatre was forced to close, marking the end of Jack's career in theatre management. This period saw the closure of many grand theatres and auditoriums. Giving rise to a new era of entertainment—the Working Men's Club scene of the late 1950s and 1960s, where live performances merged with beer, tobacco, and bingo.

Ironically, this very shift in entertainment became the foundation of a successful career for Jack and Rita's only son, Martin. He carved out a long and successful career as a drummer and vocalist, performing with various rock and pop bands—a career that sustained him from his teen years to his seventies.

Rita and Jack remained happily married for the rest of their days. Sharing their love of music, dance and theatre with their family, friends and grandchildren.

Rita's sister Betty married, enjoying children and grandchildren, and the sisters remained very close, moving back together to Hull in their later years.

As far as we know, there is very little formal recognition dedicated to the Entertainments National Service Association (ENSA) and the role its performers played during World War II. Despite its efforts to support wellbeing and morale—bringing music, comedy, and theatre to troops during those years—there are very few museum exhibitions, archives, or dedicated collections preserving ENSA's history.

While some war museums and theatre archives acknowledge ENSA's contributions, no major institution has fully captured the scale, sacrifices, and achievements of the performers who travelled across the world, often risking their lives, to bring comfort and entertainment to those serving in wartime.

The stories of singers, actors, comedians, and musicians who kept spirits high in the darkest of times deserve to be preserved and celebrated. This would ensure that future generations understand the cultural and historical significance of ENSA's work. Publishing Rita's memoir is our attempt to preserve and share this work. Not just for our Mum, Nana and Aunt, but for the countless other performers.

If you enjoyed reading this book, please consider sharing it to spread the word of the work of ENSA or leave a review to help ensure this book remains available for others to read.

Rita

www.ingramcontent.com/pod-product-compliance
Ingram Content Group UK Ltd.
Pitfield, Milton Keynes, MK11 3LW, UK
UKHW051308270525
6099UKWH00040B/1360